GW00507643

RA

NT!

✵❋⚡/*@

contents

introduction

As the world rolls slowly on towards its almost certain **doom**, we leave far behind us the gentler era of our parents and our grandparents, that era in which restraint was a virtue and saying exactly what one thought was simply not *comme il faut*. Better to count to ten, bite one's lip, swallow one's bile – even if it burnt one's gorge to a crisp and popped one's eyes from one's sockets.

But now, egged on by **californicated** psychobabblers and 12-year-old Reality TV producers, we are compelled – to use the jargon – to 'let it all hang out'. Anger is given free rein, tongues are unheld, the dogs of war are let loose to savage the ankles of any who cross us, or even annoy us just the tiniest wee bit. The devil damn thee black, we cry, and launch into excesses of vituperation, harangues of hurtfulness, floods of **filth**. Sticks and stones …

Have we all succumbed to that most fashionable of complaints, Intermittent **Explosive** Disorder? In America, according to researchers at Harvard Medical School and Chicago University, as many as 16 million people – 4 per cent of the population – have

been diagnosed with IED. To qualify, one must have had, in a single year, 'three episodes of impulsive **aggressiveness** which are grossly out of proportion to the situation'.

The problem is not confined to America. As this modest volume goes to press, ill-tempered queues are forming outside IED clinics all over the country – **seething** hordes of footballers, footballers' wives, football managers, football journalists, tabloid columnists, InterWeb bloggers, chatroom flamers, angry young women, grumpy old men, 'alternative' comedians, petulant politicians, shock jocks, supermodels, testosterone junkies, preening popsters, TV chefs, soap stars, D-list celebs (but we repeat ourselves) – the whole self-regarding, potty-mouthed, **talentless**, time-wasting bunch of them, whose intemperate outpourings fill the pages that follow. And to whom we are, of course, immeasurably and eternally grateful.

Ivor Gripe
Isle of Dogs
September 2009

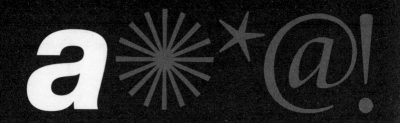

From
Abuse
to
Australians

Abuse You dirty, stuck-up, sadistic, shit-eating, cocksucking, buttfucking, penis-smelling, crotch-grabbing, ball-licking, semen-drinking, dog-raping, Nazi-loving, child-touching, cow-humping, perverted, spineless, heartless, mindless, dickless, testicle-choking, urine-gargling, jerk-offing, horse-face, sheep-fondling, toilet-kissing, self-centered, faeces-puking, dildo-shoving, snot-spitting, crap-gathering, big-nose, monkey-slapping, bastard-screwing, bead-shitting, fart-knocking, sack-busting, splooge-tasting, bear-blowing, head-swallowing, bitch-snatching, hand-jobbing, donkey-caressing, mucus-spewing, anal-plugging, ho-grabbing, uncircumsized, sewer-sipping, whoremongering, piss-swimming, midget-munching, douche bag, ho-biting, carnivorous mail order prostituting ASSHOLE! An attack launched by the Web character 'the Nostalgia Critic', created by **Doug Walker**, on another fictional Web character, 'the Angry Video Game Nerd', created by **James D. Rolfe**, as part of an ongoing cyber feud

Accountants Our experts describe you as an appallingly dull fellow, unimaginative, timid, spineless, easily dominated, no sense of humour, tedious company and irrepressibly drab and awful. And whereas in most professions these would be considered drawbacks, in accountancy they are a positive boon. And Now For Something Completely Different (1971 Monty Python film)

Tedious company and irrepressibly drab and awful

Advice If you wind up with a boring, miserable life because you listened to your mom, your dad, your teacher, your priest or some guy on TV telling you how to do your shit, then YOU DESERVE IT. **Frank Zappa** (with Peter Occhiogrosso), *The Real Frank Zappa Book* (1989)

Africa Why the hell do I want to go
to a place like Mombasa? … I just see
myself in a pot of boiling water with all
these natives dancing around me.
Mel Lastman, mayor of Toronto, referring to a planned
trip to Africa as part of his city's bid to host the Olympic
Games in 2008, quoted in the *Guardian*, 30 June 2001

*Why the
hell do I want
to go to
a place like
Mombasa?*

Air Travel There's nowhere I want to visit so much I'm
willing to be fired towards it at 700 mph in a tin can full of other
people's farts. **Frankie Boyle**

My flight to New York was delayed for 45 minutes while they
removed the luggage of a woman who'd called a security guard
an arsehole. We … prayed it was the bitch from first class with the
£4,000 bag. I bet she was livid for getting turfed off an aeroplane,
having to be told off by a customer anger
facilitator and spending another four
hours in an airport, all for calling some
big bloke in a uniform an arsehole.
If she'd known, at least she could have
called him a suppurating sphincter-
faced poxed toothpick-pricked moronic
dribbling lackey loser of an arsehole.
A.A. Gill, in the *Sunday Times*, 22 March 2009

*A suppurating
sphincter-
faced … moronic
dribbling lackey
loser*

America and Americans Go back to bed,
America. Your government has figured out how it all transpired.
Go back to bed, America. Your government is in control again.
Here. Here's *American Gladiators.* Watch this, shut up. Go back

Lily Allen vs **Elton John** In September 2008
Elton John and Lily Allen were co-hosting the *GQ* Men
of the Year Awards, when Allen announced they were
coming to 'the most important part of the night'.

Elton John: What? Are you going to have another drink?
Lily Allen: Fuck off, Elton. I am forty years younger than you
and have my whole life ahead of me!
Elton John: I could still snort you under the table.
Lily Allen: Fuck off. I don't know what you're talking about.

to bed, America. Here is *American Gladiators*. Here is 56 channels
of it! Watch these pituitary retards bang their fucking skulls
together and congratulate you on living in the land of freedom.
Here you go, America! You are free to do what we tell you! You are
free to do what we tell you! US satirist **Bill Hicks**, in *Revelations* (1992)

We have become a Nazi monster in the eyes of the whole world,
a nation of bullies and bastards who would rather kill than live
peacefully. We are not just whores for power and oil, but killer
whores with hate and fear in our hearts. We are human scum,
and that is how history will judge us. No redeeming social value.
Just whores. Get out of our way, or we'll kill you. Who does vote
for these dishonest shitheads? Who among us can be happy and
proud of having all this innocent blood on our hands? Who are
these swine? These flag-sucking half-wits who get fleeced and
fooled by stupid little rich kids like George Bush? They are the
same ones who wanted to have Muhammad Ali locked up for
refusing to kill gooks. They speak for all that is cruel and ⊙ page 18

The World's Best-Ever Complaint Letter?

Dear Mr Branson

REF: Mumbai to Heathrow 7th December 2008

I love the Virgin brand, I really do which is why I continue to use it despite a series of unfortunate incidents over the last few years. This latest incident takes the biscuit.

Ironically, by the end of the flight I would have gladly paid over a thousand rupees for a single biscuit following the culinary journey of hell I was subjected to at the hands of your corporation.

Look at this, Richard. Just look at it: [photo of strange, amorphous foodstuffs] I imagine the same questions are racing through your brilliant mind as were racing through mine on that fateful day. What is this? Why have I been given it? What have I done to deserve this? And, which one is the starter, which one is the dessert?

You don't get to a position like yours, Richard, with anything less than a generous sprinkling of observational power so I KNOW you will have spotted the tomato next to the two yellow shafts of sponge on the left. Yes, it's next to the sponge shaft without the green paste. That's got to be the clue, hasn't it? No sane person would serve a dessert with a tomato would they? Well answer me this, Richard, what sort of animal would serve a dessert with peas in? [photo of said dessert]

I know it looks like a baaji but it's

What sort of animal would serve a dessert with peas in?

in custard, Richard, custard. It must be the pudding. Well you'll be fascinated to hear that it wasn't custard. It was a sour gel with a clear oil on top. Its only redeeming feature was that it managed to be so alien to my palate that it took away the taste of the curry emanating from our miscellaneous central cuboid of beige matter. Perhaps the meal on the left might be the dessert after all.

It's your hamster in the box and it's not breathing

Anyway, this is all irrelevant at the moment. I was raised strictly but neatly by my parents and if they knew I had started dessert before the main course, a sponge shaft would be the least of my worries. So let's peel back the tin-foil on the main dish and see what's on offer.

I'll try and explain how this felt. Imagine being a 12-year-old boy, Richard. Now imagine it's Christmas morning and you're sat there with your final present to open. It's a big one, and you know what it is. It's that Goodmans stereo you picked out the catalogue and wrote to Santa about.

Only you open the present and it's not in there. It's your hamster, Richard. It's your hamster in the box and it's not breathing. That's how I felt when I peeled back the foil and saw this: [photo of yellow gunk with red and green bits at the side]

Now I know what you're thinking. You're thinking it's more of that baaji custard. I admit I thought the same too, but no. It's mustard, Richard. MUSTARD. More mustard than any man could consume in a month. On the left we have a piece of broccoli and some peppers in a brown glue-like oil and on the right the

The World's Best-Ever Complaint Letter? (continued)

chef had prepared some mashed potato. The potato masher had obviously broken and so it was decided the next best thing would be to pass the potatoes through the digestive tract of a bird.

Once it was regurgitated it was clearly then blended and mixed with a bit of mustard. Everybody likes a bit of mustard, Richard.

A crime against bloody cooking ...

By now I was actually starting to feel a little hypoglycaemic. I needed a sugar hit. Luckily there was a small cookie provided. It had caught my eye earlier due to its baffling presentation: [another photo]

It appears to be in an evidence bag from the scene of a crime. A CRIME AGAINST BLOODY COOKING. Either that or some sort of back-street underground cookie, purchased off a gun-toting maniac high on his own supply of yeast. You certainly wouldn't want to be caught carrying one of these through customs. Imagine biting into a piece of brass, Richard. That would be softer on the teeth than the specimen above.

I was exhausted. All I wanted to do was relax but obviously I had to sit with that mess in front of me for half an hour. I swear the sponge shafts moved at one point. Once cleared, I decided to relax with a bit of your world-famous onboard entertainment. I switched it on: [photo of blurred face on TV screen]

I apologize for the quality of the photo, it's just it was incredibly hard to capture Boris Johnson's face through the flickering white lines running up and down the screen. Perhaps it would be better on another channel: [even more blurred image]

Is that Ray Liotta? A question I found myself asking over and over again throughout the gruelling half-hour I attempted to watch the film like this. After that I switched off. I'd had enough. I was the hungriest I'd been in my adult life and I had a splitting headache from squinting at a crackling screen.

My only option was to simply stare at the seat in front and wait for either food, or sleep. Neither came for an incredibly long time. But when it did it surpassed my wildest expectations: [photo of various plastic-wrapped items] Yes! It's another crime-scene cookie. Only this time you dunk it in the white stuff.

Richard … What is that white stuff? It looked like it was going to be yoghurt. It finally dawned on me what it was after staring at it. It was a mixture between the baaji custard and the mustard sauce. It reminded me of my first week at university. I had overheard that you could make a drink by mixing vodka and refreshers. I lied to my new friends and told them I'd done it loads of times. When I attempted to make the drink in a big bowl it formed a cheese, Richard, a cheese. That cheese looked a lot like your baaji-mustard.

So that was that, Richard. I didn't eat a bloody thing.

So that was that, Richard. I didn't eat a bloody thing

My only question is: How can you live like this? I can't imagine what dinner round your house is like, it must be like something out of a nature documentary.

As I said at the start I love your brand, I really do. It's just a shame such a simple thing could bring it crashing to its knees and begging for sustenance.

Yours sincerely   XXXX

Muhammad Ali

US boxer

Of Floyd Patterson, before their 1965 fight:
He's a deaf-dumb so-called Negro who needs a spanking.
I plan to punish him for the things he said, cause him pain …
The little old pork-chop eater don't have a chance.

Patterson, a Catholic, had said,
'The image of a Black Muslim as the world heavyweight champion disgraces the sport and the nation.'

I'm going to beat your Christian ass, you white flag-waving son of a bitch!

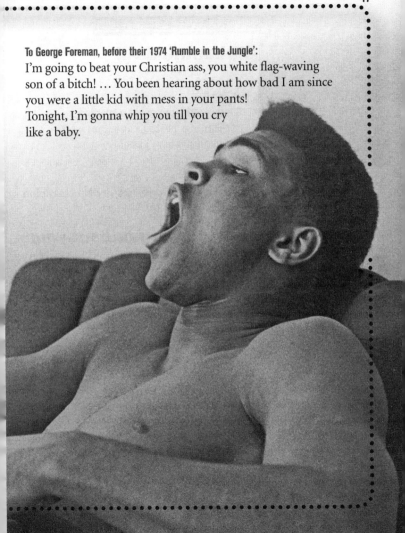

To George Foreman, before their 1974 'Rumble in the Jungle':
I'm going to beat your Christian ass, you white flag-waving son of a bitch! … You been hearing about how bad I am since you were a little kid with mess in your pants! Tonight, I'm gonna whip you till you cry like a baby.

stupid and vicious in the American character. They are the racists and hate mongers among us; they are the Ku Klux Klan. I piss down the throats of these Nazis. And I am too old to worry about whether they like it or not. Fuck them. **Hunter S. Thompson,** *Kingdom of Fear: Loathsome Secrets of a Star-crossed Child in the Final Days of the American Century* (2004)

> *Bullies and bastards ... flag-sucking half-wits*

Let us be painfully honest about it. Yes, they are repulsive people, charmless, rude, cocky, mercenary, humourless, ugly, full of nauseatingly fake religiosity, and as odious in victory as they are unsporting in defeat. **Matthew Norman,** in the *Evening Standard*, 1999, after American spectators flooded the green in premature celebration of victory in that year's Ryder Cup

If you travel to the States … they have a lot of different words than like what we use. For instance: they say 'elevator', we say 'lift'; they say 'drapes', we say 'curtains'; they say 'president', we say 'seriously deranged git'. **Alexei Sayle**

> *They say 'president', we say 'seriously deranged git'*

We are a violent society. Our foreign policy is based on violence. Barack Obama is out there, being this charming, incredibly warm human being, and you know as well as I do, that he represents a nation whose primary directive is kill. Kill, loot, pillage, take. You don't believe that? Then let me ask you something. Does

Cuba have a military presence in 140 countries? No. Does Russia?
No. Does China? No. Does – go ahead, pick one! Go ahead! There's
one country on earth that has a military presence in 140 countries.
And it's us. And why do we have it there? Why do we have them
there? This is a violent society! Liberal US talk-show host **Mike Malloy**, 3 April 2009

Americans would rather live next to a pervert heroin addict
Communist pornographer than a person with an unkempt
lawn. **Dave Barry**, *The Taming of the Screw* (1983)

That 'God Damn America' Sermon

When it came to treating her citizens of African descent
fairly, America failed. She put them in chains, the
government put them on slave quarters, put them on
auction blocks, put them in cotton field, put them in inferior
schools, put them in substandard housing, put them in
scientific experiments, put them in the lowest paying jobs,
put them outside the equal protection of the law, kept them
out of their racist bastions of higher education and locked
them into positions of hopelessness and helplessness. The
government gives them the drugs, builds bigger prisons,
passes a three-strike law and then wants us to sing 'God Bless
America.' No, no, no, not God Bless America. God damn
America – that's in the Bible – for killing innocent people.
God damn America, for treating our citizens as less than
human. God damn America, as long as she tries to act like
she is God, and she is supreme. **Jeremiah Wright**, retired pastor at
Barack Obama's church in Chicago

Idi Amin
Former Ugandan dictator   Amin? He's just a goddamn cannibal. A goddamn cannibal asshole. He'd eat his own mother. Christ! He'd eat his own grandmother! US president **Richard Nixon**

Martin Amis
English novelist   Being short, shagging, smoking fags – far more people know Amis for these things than have read his novels, and perhaps this is appropriate, despite his wails of anguish, for he is obviously much better at these things than at writing novels … What a clogged-up, clod-hopping, plate-juggling great show-off he is, and what a relief it is not to have to read his books any more in case you get laughed at down the Soho Brasserie … A lightweight mind attempting to grapple with heavyweight matters is one of the most wretched spectacles metropolitan life has to offer. If only he'd stuck to writing about smoking, shagging and snooker, on the other hand, he might even have been the next Nick Hornby. **Julie Burchill**, reviewing Amis's 1999 autobiography *Experience* in the *Spectator*

> **A clogged-up, clod-hopping, plate-juggling great show-off**

Animals
I do not like animals. Of any sort. I don't even like the idea of animals. Animals are no friends of mine. They are not welcome in my house. They occupy no space in my heart. Animals are off my list. I might more accurately state that I do not like animals, with two exceptions. The first being in the past tense, at which point I like them just fine, in the form of nice crispy spareribs and Bass Weejun penny loafers. And the second

being outside, by which I mean not merely outside the house, but genuinely outside, as in outside in the woods, or preferably outside in the South American jungle. This is, after all, only fair. I don't go there; why should they come here? **Fran Lebowitz**, *Social Studies* (1981)

In just a month after animals were released, they would be back in animal prison for trespassing, failure to pay their taxes, assaulting people and each other, and for fucking and shitting all over the shitty, fucking place! **Penn Fraser Jillette**, on the TV show *Penn & Teller: Bullshit!*

Animals ... fucking and shitting all over the shitty, fucking place!

Animal Rights Activists The PETA [People for the Ethical Treatment of Animals] you don't know would outlaw fishing, circuses, dog shows, horseback riding and zoos. They even oppose using service animals like eye-dogs for the blind. Fucking blind bastards torturing those dogs! In PETA, there's no room for Kentucky Fried Chicken, or the Kentucky Derby ... And pets are forbidden in PETA's world too. That's right! No pets. Hey all you pet lovers who donate to PETA, feel like a sucker yet? **Penn Fraser Jillette**, on the TV show *Penn & Teller: Bullshit!*

Apologies Tony Blair ... followed the example of Bill Clinton, who apologised for slavery, by apologising for the Irish potato famine. And what do those historical events have in common? This: neither Clinton nor Blair were there. They had nothing to do with it. They weren't even born. They were spotless. Blameless. You might as well ask me to apologise for the Amritsar massacre, or the Crusades, or the explosion of Krakatoa. An apology for something you didn't do is a meaningless apology … When people apologise for something they haven't done, then you know you're being conned.

Simon Hoggart, grumpieroldmen.co.uk,
15 April 2005

The Apprentice

This year's contestants are a tidy assortment of recruitment filth who take you right back to the Eighties. It's as if dinosaur-cloning scientists merged the DNA of Margaret Thatcher, Gordon Gecko and Alan B'stard and spawned an unholy litter of goal-orientated careerist scum in one go.

aerialtelly.co.uk (see also Alan Sugar)

An unholy litter of goal-orientated careerist scum

Ask yourself: would you rather have a glass of wine with lippy Saira Khan from *The Apprentice* or spend a day removing your own spleen with a purloined grab-claw from one of those pier arcade things that don't let you pick up the fake watch? The correct answer is, of course: Left. Stop. Forward. Stop. Damn. Left. Ouch. Right. Stop … **Euan Ferguson**, in the *Observer*,
24 September 2006

Aristocrats Historical throwbacks and hillbilly inbreds.
Tony McNulty, Labour MP, on hereditary peers

Of the House of Lords: An ermine-lined dustbin, an up-market geriatric home with a faint smell of urine. **Austin Mitchell**, Labour MP

Arsenal FC A load of posturing French ponces wearing gloves. **Matthew Norman**, in the *Evening Standard*, 24 January 2005

Astrology People ask me what sign I am and I say, 'Faeces!' and they change the subject.
John Waters, 1992

Most people will say of astrology, 'Well, it's harmless fun.' And I should say that for 80 per cent of the cases it probably is harmless fun, but there's a strong way in which it isn't harmless. One, because it is so anti-science. You will hear things like, 'Science doesn't know everything.' Well, of course science doesn't know everything. *But, because science doesn't know everything, it doesn't mean that science knows nothing.* Science knows enough for us to be watched by a few million people now on television, for these lights to be working, for quite extraordinary miracles to have taken place in terms of the harnessing of the physical world and our dim approaches towards understanding it … **Stephen Fry**, on *Room 101*

People ask me what sign I am and I say, 'Faeces!'

Australians

All Australians are an uneducated and unruly mob. **Douglas Jardine**, England cricket captain during the 'Bodyline' tour of 1932–3. The England tour manager said that Jardine was 'a queer fellow. When he sees a cricket ground with an Australian on it, he goes mad.'

Racial characteristics: violently loud alcoholic roughnecks whose idea of fun is to throw up on your car. The national sport is breaking furniture and the average daily consumption of beer in Sydney is ten and three quarters imperial gallons for children under the age of nine. **P.J. O'Rourke**, 'Foreigners Around the World', in *National Lampoon*, 1976

Sing 'em muck – it's all they understand

So you're going to Australia? What are you going to sing? All I can say is sing 'em muck – it's all they understand. **Dame Nellie Melba**, to fellow singer Clara Butt

Whingeing Pommy Bastards

Pass a law to give every single whingeing bloody Pommy his fare home to England. Back to the smoke and the sun shining ten days a year and shit in the streets. Yer can have it. **Thomas Keneally**, *The Chant of Jimmie Blacksmith* (1972)

What's with the Poms whingeing about the Wallabies whingeing? They do more whingeing about our whingeing than what we actually whinge. Letter to the *Sydney Morning Herald*, November 2003, during the Rugby World Cup

Racial characteristics:
violently loud alcoholic roughnecks whose idea of fun is to throw up on your car

From
BBC
to
Bush

The BBC Working for it has always been a bit like living in Stalin's Russia, with one five-year-plan, one resoundingly empty slogan after another. One BBC, Making it Happen, Creative Futures, they all blur into one great vacuous blur. I can't even recall what the current one is. Rather like Stalin's Russia, they express a belief that the system will go on forever ... I think it foolish to be too confident on that score. I guess there'll certainly be one more licence fee settlement. But can we really be certain there'll be a fourth? Or a fifth? ... The idea of a tax on the ownership of a television belongs in the 1950s. Why not tax people for owning a washing machine to fund the manufacture of Persil? **Jeremy Paxman**, from his James MacTaggart memorial lecture at the Media Guardian Edinburgh International Television Festival, August 2007

Let Paxman actually hit people

Poach Trisha from ITV and lock her in a windowless room full of clueless council estate scumbags ... Outdo ITV with new, ultra-cruel reality shows ... Televised hangings for licence-fee dodgers ... Let Paxman actually hit people. **Charlie Brooker** suggests ways to improve the BBC, in the *Guardian*, 29 May 2004

The Beatles The Beatles are not merely awful, I would consider it sacrilegious to say anything less than that they are godawful. They are so unbelievably horrible, so appallingly unmusical, so dogmatically insensitive to the magic of the art, that they qualify as crowned heads of anti-music, even as the imposter popes went down in history as 'anti-popes'. **William F. Buckley, Jr.**

That Christian Bale Rant in Full

The actor was upset by the activities of a member of the crew during filming of a scene from the new *Terminator* movie in February 2009.

Christian Bale: Am I going to walk around and rip your fucking lights down, in the middle of a scene? Then why the fuck are you walking right through? Ah-da-da-dah, like this in the background. What the fuck is it with you? What don't you fucking understand? You got any fucking idea about, hey, it's fucking distracting having somebody walking up behind Bryce in the middle of the fucking scene? Give me a fucking answer! What don't you get about it?

Shane Hurlbut: I was looking at the light.

Bale: Ohhhhh, goooood for you. And how was it? I hope it was fucking good, because it's useless now, isn't it?

Hurlbut: OK.

Bale: Fuck's sake man, you're amateur. McG, you got fucking something to say to this prick?

Director Joseph 'McG' McGinty Nichol: I didn't see it happen.

Bale: Well, somebody should be fucking watching and keeping an eye on him.

McG: Fair enough.

Bale: It's the second time that he doesn't give a fuck about what is going on in front of the camera, all right? I'm trying to fucking do a scene here, and I am going 'Why the fuck is Shane walking in there? What is he doing there?' Do you understand my mind is not in the scene if you're doing that?

Hurlbut: I absolutely apologize. I'm sorry, I did not mean anything by it.

Bale: Stay off the fucking set man. For fuck's sake. Alright, let's go again.

McG: Let's just take a minute.

Bale: Let's not take a fucking minute, let's go again. I'm going to fucking kick your fucking ass if you don't shut up for a second! All right?

Unknown voices: Christian, Christian. It's cool.

Bale: I'm going to go ... Do you want me to fucking go trash your lights? Do you want me to fucking trash 'em? Then why are you trashing my scene?

Hurlbut: I'm not trying to trash your scene.

Bale: You are trashing my scene!

Hurlbut: Christian, I was only ...

Bale: You do it one more fucking time and I ain't walking on this set if you're still hired. I'm fucking serious. You're a nice guy. You're a nice guy, but that don't fucking cut it when you're fucking around like this on set.

The Beautiful People

I have an important message to deliver to all the cute people all over the world. If you're out there and you're cute, maybe you're beautiful. I just want to tell you somethin' – there's more of us UGLY MOTHERFUCKERS than you are, hey-y, so watch out. **Frank Zappa**, 'Dance Contest', on the album *Tinsel Town Rebellion* (1981)

David Beckham

English footballer and fashion icon This Gaultier-saronged, Posh Spiced, Cooled Britannia, look-at-me, what-a-lad, sex-and-shopping, fame-schooled, daytime-TV, over-coiffed twerp … **The** *Daily Telegraph*, following Beckham's sending-off in England's 1998 World Cup match against Argentina

A grossly overrated player, a speechless fop with legs as bandy as a northern jockey's. **Willie Donaldson**, *I'm Leaving You Simon, You Disgust Me* (2003)

Victoria Beckham

WAG and former Spice Girl David Beckham is a national treasure because he cheated on his wife, who I understand is very, very rude. I've never met her but I always ask taxi drivers, limo drivers and airport cleaners and always the same names come up – and she is right up on top of the list … I hope he screws everything that's not tied down. **Joan Rivers**, interviewed in *Attitude* magazine, quoted on Mirror.co.uk, 26 July 2005

Kate Beckinsale

English actress Kate Beckinsale seems perfectly inoffensive, on the surface – she's not bad to look at … and she's English, which is always nice. But it's exactly this inoffensiveness that makes her worthy of scorn … Most of all, I hate Kate Beckinsale for the scene at the end of *Van Helsing* in which, after enduring what felt like hours of monster movie mash-up, we were treated to the ridiculous image of A CLOUD MADE OF KATE BECKINSALE'S FACE. It's one of the single stupidest things ever put in a movie not called *Aquanoids*, and although I know she had nothing to do with the writing, directing or visual effects involved in that scene, I can't help but throw up in my mouth a little every time I see her just out of sheer association. Curse your cloudy face, Kate Beckinsale. Curse it. **Adam Swiderski**, 'Why you should hate Kate Beckinsale', ugo.com

I can't help but throw up in my mouth a little every time I see her

Bed and Breakfasts

Oh God, the bed and breakfast! Why is it that British people can't cope with the idea of the paying guest? It's like you pay these people to stay there but you try and act as inconspicuous as you possibly can. It's like no financial transaction's taken place. It's as though you've just imposed yourself off the street. And they think, 'Who the fuck are

you? You've not just paid me £25 have you, to stay here?' First you try the lounge, the TV lounge. Suddenly you are in Poland, martial law, because there's a curfew. You're watching a film – the telly goes off at 11.30. A bloke standing over you shouting, 'I've got to get up at six o'clock this

Who the fuck are you? You've not just paid me £25 have you, to stay here?

morning, what time are you going to bed?'

All right, yes, we're going now, we're going now. You go up to bed with a sinking heart which sinks even further when you open the door and find 'Ugh! The MAUVE CANDLEWICK BEDSPREAD!' Now this is a bad sign because it is now on the cards that you are going to open up that bed and find MAUVE NYLON SHEETS. You get in there and it's like sleeping between two pieces of velcro. **Linda Smith**, *Linda Live*, 1986

Beggars   I don't like to see homeless people with dogs. I saw one today and he asked me for some money to buy food. Why should I give him money when he has a perfectly delicious dog standing right next to him? **Chelsea Handler**, US comedienne

You can't walk one block in any city in America without wackos and soaks spitting in your pants cuffs and homeless vagabonds gnawing at the tassels of your Foot-Joys. You can't stop at a stoplight without getting squeegeed in the kisser by practitioners of beggary – the most rapidly expanding sector of America's economy. One out of five American children are growing up needy, and 53 per cent of those kids have nothing for a dad except

a blind, microscopic, wiggle-tailed gamete that hasn't held a job
since it got to the womb. Drugs are an improvement on some of
these problems ... **P.J. O'Rourke**, 1992

Silvio Berlusconi Italian prime minister and media mogul

This pompous gaffe-a-minute buffoon truly believes he is the
most powerful man in the world ... My advice to spoof writers?
'Come to Italy – we have the biggest plonker
in the world.' **Gareth Carpenter**, 'Why I hate
Berlusconi', 5 January 2004, posted on thespoof.com

When you think about it, what
exactly is so lovable about a rich,
powerful older man surrounding
himself with half-naked girls ...
He's become grubby; a walking
midlife crisis in Vilebrequin beach
shorts. And he's 72! ... This is why

He's become grubby; a walking midlife crisis

Berlusconi should finally go – not because 'he can't keep it in his
pants', but because ... he can't be bothered to, and clearly does not
regard himself in any shape or form answerable to the 'minions'
who voted for him. In this way, Berlusconi has become the
personification of power gone rancid ... Perhaps it would be best
all around if ... he were to be quietly injected with bromide and
dragged discreetly to one side. In political and libidinal terms, it
could be viewed as a mercy killing. **Barbara Ellen**, in the *Observer*, 7 June 2009

David Blaine American magician and exhibitionist Blaine!
... Blaine! ... Blaine! ... Blaine! ... Blaine! ... Blaine!
Wankaaaaaaaaaaaa! **Marcus Brigstocke**

Arseholes of England 1

Basildon

Basildon suffers from fifty years of inbreeding (in addition to the hundreds of years of *keeping it in the family* practised by the original East-End overspill who originally populated this urban paradise). Yes, this is where even people from Lewisham are classed as 'posh talking bastards' and left with permanent imprints of Reebok trainers on their skulls. **'alexanderdelarge'**, chavtowns.co.uk, December 2005

Birmingham

An unspeakable excrescence of a city … as if God had unwisely partaken the night before of a divine Vindaloo of horrific pungency, and promptly evacuated his bowels over the West Midlands the next morning. The people pallid, corpse-like, moronic; the buildings so ugly as to induce a sense of nausea in the hapless onlooker. **Jonathan Coe**, *The Closed Circle* (2004). The opinion is that of a fictional poet in the novel.

Blackpool

Blackpool is ugly, dirty and a long way from anywhere … its sea is an open toilet, and its attractions nearly all cheap, provincial and dire … On Friday and Saturday nights it has more public toilets than anywhere else in Britain: elsewhere they call them doorways. **Bill Bryson**, *Notes from a Small Island* (1995)

Blackpool was real clutter – the buildings that were not only ugly but also foolish and flimsy, the vacationers sitting under a dark sky with their shirts off, sleeping with their mouths open, emitting hog whimpers. They were waiting for the sun to shine, but the forecast was rain for the next five months … Blackpool was perfectly

Birmingham

reflected in the swollen guts and unhealthy fat of its beer-guzzling visitors – eight million in the summer, when Lancashire closed to come here and belch. **Paul Theroux**, *The Kingdom by the Sea* (1983)

Chichester Also known as Shitchester, it is known as a 'little' city and it is 'little' in every sense, from its size to the tiny minds of its inhabitants. The place is full of arrogant, ignorant, thick ex-public-school yobs who throw their weight about, hit people and patronize/talk down to anyone they meet …
If you want to enjoy life and are a decent person, avoid this nasty, unfriendly, spiteful little dump like the plague. Don't even visit it. Just leave the nasty, insular, malicious little Tory-voting wankers who live there to stew in their own crap. **'snobbychavhater'**, chavtowns.co.uk, December 2005

Dudley A bleak concrete wasteland inhabited by serial murderers, masochists, occultists and freaks. **Patrick Thomson**, *Seeing the Wires* (2002)

Tony Blair Former New Labour prime minster It is just flipping unbelievable. He is a mixture of Harry Houdini and a greased piglet. He is barely human in his elusiveness. Nailing Blair is like trying to pin jelly to a wall. **Boris Johnson**, in the *Daily Telegraph*, 29 January 2004, in the wake of the Hutton Report's exoneration of the government over the David Kelly affair

A numbing fusillade of platitudes … his brain permanently on line to a fad lexicon … Mr Blair uses abstract nouns as a wine writer uses adjectives, filling space with a frothy concoction devoid of meaning. **Simon Jenkins**, in *The Times*

We are governed by an increasingly insulated, aggressive, undemocratic, cronyist, corrupt, dishonest and neo-Stalinist Prime Minister whose most memorable recent comment was the mind-boggling 'I only know what I believe.' **Michael Bywater**, Lost Worlds blog, 24 December 2004

I believe Tony Blair is an out-and-out rascal, terminally untrustworthy and close to being unhinged. I said from the start that there was something wrong in his head, and each passing year convinces me more strongly that this man is a pathological confidence-trickster. To the extent that he even believes what he says, he is delusional. To the extent that he does not, he is an actor whose first invention – himself – has been his only interesting role. **Matthew Parris**, in *The Times*, 18 March 2006

An out-and-out rascal, terminally untrustworthy and close to being unhinged

… the self-intoxicated pietist Bush and his moist-eyed sanctimonious friend Blair … are seemingly depraved and corrupt beyond redemption. Bush lied about Iraqi involvement in the September 11th attacks on Manhattan; Blair … do we need to say more than that Blair is having a lovely holiday in the Miami Beach pad of a Bee Gee? You know, *Bee Gee*? As in 'Stayin' Alive'? **Michael Bywater**, Lost Worlds blog, 30 December 2006

I couldn't bear that grinning, money-hungry, beaming, Cliff Richard-loving, Berlusconi-adoring, guitar-playing twat. I suppose I would say that, at the risk of being inoffensive. No, it's that beaming Christianity and that frightful wife with a mouth on a zip-fastener right round to the back of her head. And both of them obsessed with

Seemingly depraved and corrupt beyond redemption

being wealthy. And he got us into this disastrous war with Iraq because he had consulted with God. Like Bush. Well, anyone who claims to do something on the basis of a personal relationship to a non-existent deity … **Jonathan Miller**, interviewed in *The Times*, 15 July 2009

Brown on Blair

There is nothing that you could say to me now that I could ever believe. Remark reputedly addressed by **Gordon Brown** to Tony Blair

You've stolen my fucking budget. Remark reputedly addressed by **Gordon Brown** to Tony Blair

Books   Get stewed: Books are a load of crap.   **Philip Larkin**, 'A Study of Reading Habits' (1964)

Ian Botham   English cricketer   This fellow is the most overrated player I have ever seen. He looks too heavy, and the way he's been bowling out there, he wouldn't burst a paper bag.   **Harold Larwood**, former England fast bowler, during England's 1982–3 tour of Australia

A drug-crazed opium pusher. **Sarfraz Nawaz**, Pakistani bowler, following Botham's suspension for smoking cannabis, quoted in Botham's autobiography (1995)

A drug-crazed opium pusher

If you've signed the cunt, you can sack the cunt.   **Kelvin Mackenzie**, editor of the *Sun*, on firing Botham as a columnist after he lost the England captaincy in 1981. Quoted in David Hopps, *A Century of Great Cricket Quotes* (1998)

Bottled Water   How about Everest Water? ... Everest comes from the industrial section of Corpus Christi, Texas! In fact if you read the fine print on the FUCKING LABEL, they even admit that the water comes from a MUNICIPAL SOURCE! THAT IS TAP WATER, brothers and sisters of the cult of the bottle! **Penn Fraser Jillette**, on the TV show *Penn & Teller: Bullshit!*

Lee Bowyer   English footballer   Lee Bowyer is the nastiest piece of work in sport – a violent, foul-mouthed, horrible little lout.   **Piers Morgan**, in the *Evening Standard*, 5 April 2005

All promoters are pimps

Boxing

All boxers are prostitutes and all promoters are pimps. **Larry Holmes**, US boxer

I now find the whole subject of professional boxing disgusting. Except for the fighters, you're talking about human scum, nothing more. Professional boxing is utterly immoral. It's not capable of reformation. You'll never clean it up. Mud can never be clean. **Howard Cosell**, US sports journalist, in 1982, as Larry Holmes faced an outclassed Tex Cobb, and shortly after Duk Koo Kim died after a fight with Ray Mancini

Russell Brand

British stand-up comic and TV presenter

Do I really need to spell this one out? A stick insect with back-combed hair? Forsooth! A media tart without a heart, but a mouth with verbal dysentery, a worrying obsession with his own genitalia and so self-obsessed with his own image as to not realize that within a few years he will be forever replayed on nostalgia programmes as a sort of 'didn't we look like a bunch of twats in the early 2000s?' strand. **The Daily Spleen**: 'Utterly pointless celebrities', on daily-spleen.blogspot.com

A media tart without a heart, but a mouth with verbal dysentery

Gordon Brown

New Labour prime minister Gordon Brown would make an effing awful prime minister. Unnamed member of Tony Blair's cabinet speaking off the record to the BBC's political editor Nick Robinson.

We have this one-eyed Scottish idiot who keeps telling us everything's fine and he's saved the world and we know he's lying, but he's smooth at telling us. Jeremy Clarkson, on tour in Australia, February 2009

While the Prime Minister lives out his excruciating personal tragedy, we're going to have to suffer this zombie horror show for another year and endure the consequences for generations. If Gordon were a dog, he'd be put down.
Richard Littlejohn, in the *Daily Mail*, 1 May 2009

It's like being trapped in a hot room filled with an overpowering fart smell

Assailed from all directions, stumbling, bumbling, droning, punch-drunk, hapless, hopeless, and aching with palpable misery, he increasingly resembles a depressed elephant, slowly being felled by a thousand pin-sized arrows fired into his hide by a million tiny natives, still somehow moving forward, trudging wearily toward its allotted graveyard-slot with morose resignation … I can't wait for the general election – not because I want to see Prime Minister Wormface Cameron smugging his way into Downing Street, because I don't – but just because I don't think I can bear this mishap-strewn landscape a moment longer. It's like being trapped in a hot room filled with an overpowering fart smell, waiting for someone outside to come along and open the window. Charlie Brooker, in the *Guardian*, 11 May 2009

Cherie Blair's just brought out her autobiography hasn't she? If Gordon Brown's wife did the same it'd probably be less eventful than Anne Frank's. Monday, stayed in, Gordon cried. **Frankie Boyle**

Brussels Sprouts Those little balls of hell, limp and wilted after a lifetime of being pissed on by birds and other contaminated creatures. **John Waters**

Julie Burchill English columnist

On Burchill's claim to have been 'Queen of the Groucho': Any of us who have worked at the Groucho will remember Ms Burchill as a tubby woman in a scruffy blue raincoat (always buttoned up to the top) who spoke in a silly voice and who was absurdly deferential to her admittedly gorgeous husband Cosmo Landesman.

She was a far from glamorous figure. I have absolutely no recollection of her holding court, being fabulous or even having many friends or hangers-on. If there was anything remarkable about her behaviour, it was that she always seemed an uncomfortable and slightly desperate figure.

Ms Burchill needs to be careful in her rewriting of such recent history, as most of us were not so addled with coke that we can't remember that Julie Burchill's time at the Groucho was a simple matter of a fat bird in a blue mac sitting in the corner. **Deborah Bosley,** formerly head waitress at the Groucho Club, letter to the *Independent*, 18 June 2000

Her insights were, and remain, negligible, on the level of a toddler having a tantrum. I want. I hate. You're my bestest friend. You're horrid. She excoriates some poor bastard for being too old, too fat … but the sad irony is that she is too old, too fat herself.
Michael Bywater, in 1998

After our first afternoon of cold vodka and hot sex, a voice inside my head said: don't fall for this woman; she will only break your heart. After our second afternoon of cold vodka and hot sex, the voice inside my head said: don't fall for this woman; she's crazy, immoral and treacherous. After our third afternoon of cold vodka and hot sex, the voice said: don't fall for this woman. For God's sake, wake up, Cosmo, this broad is a sociopath, a Stalinist with Nietzschean tendencies who drinks like a fish and eats nice middle-class Jewish boys like you for breakfast. You have been warned: stay away! Reader, I married that woman.   **Cosmo Landesman**, Burchill's second husband, in his memoir *Starstruck: Fame, Failure, My Family and Me* (2008)

Burchill on Burchill and everybody else:

… someone who is very keen to make money and has failed will abuse me as a moneygrubber; the sex starved will call me bitter and lonely; someone who wants to be a writer and fails will abuse my talent; the hideous will say I'm ugly; and that porky pig DAWN FRENCH always says I'm fat. But insult me if it makes your own dull little lives more bearable – come on, get it all up! But don't ever mistake me for some sucker who gives a damn about your opinions, because then the laugh really is on you.
Julie Burchill, online Q&A session, guardian.co.uk, 27 April 2001

George H.W. Bush   41st President of the USA It's not that I
disagree with Bush's economic policy or his foreign policy, it's that I believe he was a child of Satan sent here to destroy the planet Earth.   US satirist **Bill Hicks**, in *Shock and Awe*, 11 November 1992

George W. Bush   43rd President of the USA A coil of intestine
in a vaudeville suit.   **Michael Bywater**, Lost Worlds blog, 3 September 2005

The President is a cross-eyed Texan warmonger, unelected, inarticulate, who epitomizes the arrogance of American foreign policy. Unsigned editorial in the *Spectator*, assumed to be by the editor **Boris Johnson**, 22 November 2003

But wow! This goofy child president we have on our hands now. He is demonstrably a fool and a failure, and this is only the summer of '03 … The US Treasury is empty, we are losing that stupid, fraudulent chickencrap war in Iraq, and every country in the world except a handful of corrupt Brits despises us. We are losers, and that is the one unforgiveable sin in America. **Hunter S. Thompson**, 'Welcome to the Big Darkness' (July 2003)

He struggles to exude authority. He furrows his brow, trying to look more sagacious, but he ends up looking as if he has indigestion. Appearing confused at his own speech, he seems like a first-grade actor in a production of *James and the Giant Peach*. Are his blinks Morse code for 'Oh, man, don't let that teleprompter break?' **Maureen Dowd**, in the *New York Times*

The Bush people have virtually got rid of Magna Carta and habeas corpus. In a normal republic I would probably have raised an army and overthrown them. It will take a hundred years to put it all back. Those neocons, lawyers, the big corporations – worse than that, extremists – want to get rid of the great power of oversight of the executive … They're crooks. They're just gangsters. They are the enemy of the United States. There's no such thing as a war on terrorism. It's idiotic. There are slogans. It's advertising, which is the only art form we've invented and developed. It's lies. **Gore Vidal**, interviewed on the *South Bank Show*, 18 May 2008

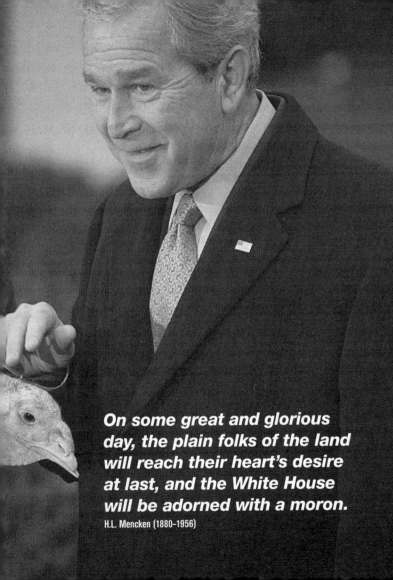

On some great and glorious day, the plain folks of the land will reach their heart's desire at last, and the White House will be adorned with a moron.

H.L. Mencken (1880–1956)

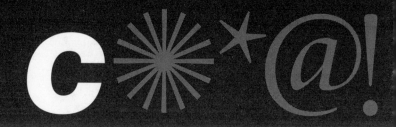

C✳*@!

From
Cameron
to
Cyclists

David Cameron

David Cameron is an idiot. A simpering, say-anything, dough-faced, preposterous waddling idiot with a feeble, insincere voice and an irritating tendency to squat near the top of opinion polls … There is nothing to him. He is like a hollow Easter egg with no bag of sweets inside. Cameron will say absolutely anything if he thinks it might get him elected … He's nothing. He's no one … So nyahh nyahh, Dave, you fair-weather, upper-crust guff-cloud. Nyahh nyahh. **Charlie Brooker**, in the *Guardian*, 2 April 2007

I'm Dave the jellyfish! My family owns half of Berkshire. My wife's family owns half of Lincolnshire. That's why I need public help to buy a special jellyfish home, otherwise I'd be nothing more than a washed-up blob of snot. **Steve Bell**, *If…* cartoon strip, in the *Guardian*, 4 June 2009

Nothing more than a washed-up blob of snot

All he does is repeatedly bleat 'change' like a tramp in a doorway, and his only stated policy is 'to become prime minister' … David Cameron is a chancer who's even more woefully unfit for government than Gordon Brown. **David Mitchell**, in the *Observer*, 14 June 2009

Caravanning

You aren't allowed to have a party, you aren't allowed to have music, you aren't allowed to play ball games, you aren't allowed to have a camp fire, you have to park within two feet of a post, you have to keep quiet, you have to be in bed by eleven. This is not a holiday, it's a concentration camp! **Jeremy Clarkson** on *Top Gear*

B-Rude

Serial Ranter no. 2

Naomi Campbell

Supermodel and tantrum-thrower

To a woman who photographed her on a flight to South Africa:
You are an ugly bitch with a head like an alien.

In 2008 Campbell threw yet another wobbly, when informed that one of her bags had not been loaded onto her LA-bound plane at Heathrow. Among her observations on that occasion, the following have been reported:
This is a joke, right? Why can't you do anything right? Get all my bags on this flight! I'm Naomi Campbell … I can't believe you have lost my fucking bag. Bring me my fucking bags now … How dare you tell me what my options are? You are not leaving until you find my fucking bags … Bloody fools! … They have lost my fucking bag, get me another flight, get hold of the press, get my lawyer … Arseholes! You're all arseholes! … You bitch, I want my luggage – it's because I'm black and famous … You are a racist, you would not be doing this if I was white … I am going to screw you, like a motherfucker … Fuck you, fuck you, Captain … It's because I'm a black woman, you are all racist, I'm going to sue you, I'm going to fuck you … You can't fucking touch me, my cousin is Scotland Yard … Fuck off, I have paid £5,000 for this. I have a right to be on this plane …

Despite her protestations, Campbell was arrested and handcuffed by armed police, and subsequently pleaded guilty to two charges of assaulting police officers and using threatening and insulting words and behaviour. She was sentenced to 200 hours of community service.

Jimmy Carr English comedian His idea of wit is a barrage of filth and the sort of humour most men grow out of in their teens. **Anne Widdecombe**, quoted in *The Times*, 24 December 2008

Jimmy Carter 39th President of the USA Carter is your typical smiling, brilliant, back-stabbing, bull-shitting Southern nut-cutter. **Lane Kirkland**, US trade union leader, in 1976

Cats Usually I know exactly what the cat has eaten. Not only have I fed it to the cat, at the cat's keen insistence, but the cat has thrown it up on the rug and someone has tracked it all the way over on to the other rug. I don't know why cats are such habitual vomiters. They don't seem to enjoy it, judging by the sounds they make while doing it. It's in their nature. A dog is going to bark. A cat is going to vomit.

Roy Blount, Jr, in *Esquire*, 1984

I can see stopping a car for a dog. But a cat? You squish a cat and go on. **James Gallagher**

Celebrity Chefs A bunch of arseholes … assembling bits of gastronomic Lego without the faintest idea where they fucking come from. **Keith Floyd**, quoted on *Mail Online*, 15 September 2009

Hugh Fearnley-Whittingstall: Goose-stuffing lifestyle glutton who has turned a smallholding in west Dorset into a slaughterhouse.
Hermione Eyre and **William Donaldson**, *The Dictionary of National Celebrity* (2005)

Ainsley Harriott: And how many versions of what is, basically, your dinner can Ainsley do? There must be executives stalking the corridors of White City thinking, 'We need a new idea for Ainsley. He's so jolly – what can we have? We've had him doing *Can't Cook, Won't Cook, Ready Steady Cook, Barbecues* – We need something new, different, edgy – How about this, we like this – *Ainsley's Death Row Dinners.*' Yes, the jolly chef tours the condemned man with a last supper to remember. We can have the recipes in the *Radio Times* – Ainsley's Humanely Fried Chicken, with a lethal injection of butter! **Linda Smith**, *Wrap Up Warm* tour, 2004

Jamie Oliver: I hate Jamie Oliver, I have many many reasons, and there isn't enough space on the web for me to log them all. His smarmy TV show, 'pucka this, pucka that', his adverts for Sainsbury's, his … cockney wanker accent – his SCOOTER, the fact that he has all his mates round to his fashionably distressed loft apartment for tapas and weak lager, 'oh look he's got a chinese friend and a black friend and a martian friend and they all look like male models' … so what if he helped kids, so what if he used his own money … I don't want young offenders cooking my dinner, same as I don't want them in my house or removing my spleen. On www.justramit.co.uk

Prince Charles Heir to the throne Prince Charles is an

insensitive, hypocritical oaf and Princess Diana is a selfish, empty-headed bimbo. They should never have got married in the first place. I blame the parents. **Richard Littlejohn**, in the *Sun*

The grovelling little bastard. **Spike Milligan**, after Charles's tribute to him was read out at the British Comedy Awards, 1994

Here is a man who swans into Cambridge with piss-poor exam results because his mother is Queen. Gets handed a nineteen-year-old virgin when he decides to get married because his mother is Queen. Will one day be head of state because his mother is Queen. A man who if forced to go into the real world and succeed on natural skill and ability would be lucky to get a job as a janitor … When that jug-eared waste of taxpayers' money actually achieves something on the basis of hard work and merit I'll be happy to listen to his opinions. In the meantime he really should keep his mouth shut and go back to killing wildlife and fucking old trout. Could we not go back to beheading these people? **'clairwil'** blog on clairwil.tripod.com

Chavs and Chavettes

Spindly little ratboys and pigdog chavettes

Legend has it that the chav virus was first discovered in this town [Chatham], and from here spread to the entire country. The Chatham Girl mutated into the Chavette we have today. This shit-hole of a town has two types of inhabitant, the pikey inbred local white trash and the knuckle-dragging squaddie cannon fodder. The lack of diversity in these two gene pools means that the local spunk buckets churn out spindly little ratboys and pigdog chavettes at an alarming rate. Most of the ratboys will be looking at a one-way ticket to a young offenders' institute, while the chavettes will generally become child mothers or crack whores. **'crowman'**, chavtowns.co.uk, November 2005

Modified Vauxhall Novas parked outside the house emitting the kind of bass that causes windows to vibrate, pre-teens giving you verbal outside Spar because you won't go in and buy them ten Bensons and gangs of lads giving you filthy looks because you have the audacity to drive along the stretch of road they want to walk down the middle of. I live in Chavsville and I don't give a stuff if it isn't politically correct to moan about 'the new British underclass', they are a bloody nuisance. **'Vik'**, on news.bbc.co.uk, January 2005

A nation of pretentious ponces

I've noticed that calling people 'chavs' says far, far more about the caller than it does the called … Thus individuals who aren't getting any good lovin' will hiss on ceaselessly about how slaggy chavs are; those who know that secretly their job is one long duck, dive'n'skive (journalists are particularly culpable here) will bang on about how idle chavs are; and those who stayed in long and expensive educations yet are earning less before tax per annum than Wayne Rooney spends on valet parking each year will be rather cross about how much money he pulls in with no help from anyone but his rather clever feet … Perhaps we are a nation of chavs – and that suits me fine, as the alternative would be being a nation of pretentious ponces. **Julie Burchill**, in *The Times*, 18 February 2005

… young men too revolting to find a nice girl and too thick to hold down a decent job, for whom the tribalism of soccer becomes both an occupation and a family. You see them hanging around towns with their cheap imitation soccer-star haircuts and their shiny wannabe soccer-star shirts – pathetic clones of pathetic idols. **Simon Heffer** in the *Daily Mail*, 2001

Chelsea FC My arms withered and my body was covered in pus-filled sores, but no matter how bad it got I consoled myself by remembering I wasn't a Chelsea fan. **Ian Holloway**, then manager of Queen's Park Rangers, tells ITV viewers in June 2005 how he endured a bout of illness

Dick Cheney Vice-president to George W. Bush So loathsome his own party is frightened of him. Manages to deliver stunning lies with an air of sneering authority. Shamelessly employs scare tactics in order to strip the federal government of any resemblance to the one described in the constitution. So visibly evil that all of the documented evidence against him is superfluous. The kind of guy who starts talking cannibalism the minute he steps on the lifeboat. *The Beast's* '50 Most Loathsome People in America 2004'

The kind of guy who starts talking cannibalism the minute he steps on the lifeboat

Did the American people actually elect this corrupt, greedy psychopath as Vice-President? Is the job title some sort of sick pun? **Michael Bywater**, Lost Worlds blog, 11 September 2005

Children Here's another idea that should be punctured, the idea that childbirth is a miracle. I don't know who started this rumour but it's not a miracle. No more a miracle than eating food and a turd coming out of your butt. It's a chemical reaction and a biological reaction. You want to know a miracle? A miracle is raising a kid that doesn't talk in a fucking movie theatre ... I'll go you one further, and this is the routine that has virtually ended my career in America. If you have children here tonight – and I assume some of you do – I am sorry to tell you this. They are not special. I'll let that sink in. Don't get me wrong, folks. I know you think they're special. You think that. I'm telling you – they're not. Did you know that every time a guy comes, he comes 200 million sperm? Did you know that? And you mean to tell me you think your child is special? Because one out of 200 million sperm connected ... Gee, what are the fucking odds? Do you know what that means? I have wiped entire civilizations off of my chest, with a grey gym sock. That is special. Entire nations have flaked and crusted in the hair around my navel. That is special. And I want you to think about that, you two-egg-carrying beings out there with that holier-than-thou, we-have-the-gift-of-life attitude. I have tossed universes, in my underpants, while napping. That is special. US satirist **Bill Hicks**, from *Sane Man* (1989)

I don't know how perverts stand it

My hero is Good King Herod. I have never understood child molestation because in order to molest a child, you have to be in the same room with a child, and I don't know how perverts stand it. **Florence King**, 'the thinking man's redneck', 1992

Christmas
I return your seasonal greeting card with contempt. May your hypocritical words choke you and may they choke you early in the New Year. Ulster Unionist politician **Kennedy Lindsay**, returning a Christmas card from Garret FitzGerald, Irish minister of foreign affairs, in the 1970s

May your hypocritical words choke you ...

Did you ever notice, the only one in *A Christmas Carol* with any character is Scrooge? Marley is a whiner who fucked over the world and then hadn't the spine to pay his dues quietly; Belle, Scrooge's ex-girlfriend, deserted him when he needed her most; Bob Cratchit is a gutless toady without enough get-up-and-go to assert himself; and the less said about that little treacle-mouth, Tiny Tim, the better. **Harlan Ellison**

Early in life I developed a distaste for the Cratchits that time has not sweetened. I do not think I was an embittered child, but the Cratchits' aggressive worthiness, their exultation over that wretched goose, disgusted me. I particularly disliked Tiny Tim (a part always played by a girl because girls had superior powers of looking moribund and worthy at the same time), and when he chirped, 'God bless us every one!' my mental response was akin to Sam Goldwyn's famous phrase, 'Include me out.' **Robertson Davies**, Canadian novelist

Jeremy Clarkson
Motoring journalist I'll be entirely frank, I don't like Jeremy Clarkson very much. I suspect that at some point early in his life, he decided that it was necessary for someone to remind us that the French are smelly, that BMWs ➲ page 60

Clarkson on Cars

On small cars:

We all know that small cars are good for us. But so is cod liver oil.
And jogging. On *Top Gear*

On supercars:

Supercars are supposed to run over Arthur Scargill and then run
over him again for good measure. They are designed to melt ice
caps, kill the poor, poison the water table, destroy the ozone layer,
decimate indigenous wildlife, recapture the Falkland Islands and
turn the entire third world into a huge uninhabitable desert.
On *Top Gear*

On the Maserati Quattroporte:

In a list of the five most rubbish things in the world, I'd have
America's foreign policy at five. AIDS at four. Iran's nuclear
programme at three. Gordon Brown at two and Maserati's gearbox
at number one. It is that bad. In the *Sunday Times,* 9 July 2006

On the Nissan Almera:

Telling people at a dinner party you drive a Nissan Almera is
like telling them you've got the ebola virus and you're about to
sneeze. On *Top Gear*

On the Peugeot 407 Coupé 2.7 V6 HDi SE:

It has the zip of a chairlift. With plodding performance and
steady-as-she-goes handling the only thing this car will make you
feel like is a cup of Horlicks with a splash of hemlock. Empty-
nesters should buy a PlayStation instead, and spend the afternoon
shooting crack whores. In the *Times online,* 19 March 2006

On the Perodua Kelisa:

This is without doubt the worst car, not just in its category but in the world … The Malaysian-made Kelisa has a top speed of 88mph but takes so long to reach it that no one has ever lived long enough to verify the claim. It only has three cylinders, the inside is tackier than Anthea Turner's wedding and you don't want to think what would happen if it bumped into a lamppost. Also, its name sounds like a disease … Cars like the Kelisa are for African taxi drivers, a rival for the moped and the mule. In *The Times*, 2 February 2008

On the Kia Rio:

You may have seen *The Fly II*, in which a scientist attempts to teleport a dog. In one of the most gruesome scenes I've seen in a film it arrives at its destination completely inside out. Well the Rio is uglier than that. Inside, things get worse … After three days of being transported in the Rio, my kids thought it was a brilliant idea to walk instead. Even though their school is 18 miles away and it was blowing a gale directly from the Canadian tundra. In the *Sunday Times*, 15 February 2004

On the Mitsubishi Warrior:

'What,' I exclaimed, 'in the name of all that's holy, do we want one of those for?' We're European. We were sipping tea while the Americans were shooting Indians. We've had 2,000 years to get used to civilisation, not 20 minutes. We're advanced, we're slim, we're at the cutting edge of evolution. We think that shooting bears is daft. Budweiser gives us a headache and we think George Bush is an arse. 'So why in God's name do we want to drive around in a car made from a hen house and two bits of railway track?' In the *Sunday Times*, 30 May 2004

are Nazi staff cars and that Italians are as crooked as a dog's hind leg. He has adopted a personality that, as an Englishman, suggests he would have been happier with Queen Victoria on the throne and with an Empire that stretched from London to the far reaches of the globe rather than Blair and the Scottish having their own parliament. He is a friend of A.A. Gill, the toadying columnist who would be damned to Hell for all of eternity were there only an eighth deadly sin for smugness. He is, as he is often fond of pointing out about cars that he dislikes, rather pointless.

Eamonn McCusker, review of Clarkson's DVD *Heaven and Hell* on dvd times.co.uk

JEREMY CLARKSON'S A TOP GIT

Boorish Jeremy Clarkson is the posh version of an English knuckle-trailing thug ... If this tosser doesn't express proper regret – as opposed to the half-baked 'apology' he reluctantly made – I'm stopping paying my licence fee. **Anna Smith**, in the *Daily Mirror*, 8 February 2009, following Clarkson's attack on Gordon Brown (see page 40).

The posh version of an English knuckle-trailing thug

Bill Clinton 42nd President of the USA We're now at the point that it's beyond whether or not this guy is a horny hick. I really think it's a question of his mental stability. He really could be a lunatic. I think it is a rational question for Americans to ask whether their president is insane. Rightwing commentator **Ann Coulter**

If the President's penis is straight, it is the only thing about his administration that is. **Mark Steyn**

Not only do you kick him, you kick him until he passes out

When Clinton was summoned to appear before a grand jury during the Lewinsky scandal:

This whole thing about not kicking someone when they are down is BS. Not only do you kick him, you kick him until he passes out – then beat him over the head with a baseball bat, then roll him up in an old rug, and throw him off the cliff into the pound[ing] surf below!!!! **Michael Scanlon**, Republican PR man

On Clinton working with George Bush Snr and George W. Bush after the Hurricane Katrina disaster:

This Democratic whore, Bill Clinton – all of a sudden, I can't stand him anymore. To me, he is as corrupt and degenerate as the Bushes. He has become almost like an associate of the Bush Crime Family … I've had enough of this son of a bitch. I've had enough of him, and his crazy-ass wife. I've had enough, OK? The Clintons can go straight to Hell, along with the Bushes. I've had enough of Bill Clinton; I've had it with this guy … I'll say it again: Why isn't Clinton grabbing them by their neckties and shaking them until both these old bastards' teeth rattle out of their mouths, about why they have destroyed the United States? But that's not Clinton. Liberal US talk-show host **Mike Malloy**, 9 January 2005

Hillary Clinton Former first lady and presidential contender

She is a brittle, relentless manipulator with few stable core values who shuffles through useful personalities like a card shark ('Cue the tears!'). Forget all her little gold crosses: Hillary's real god is political expediency. Do Americans truly want this hard-bitten Machiavellian back in the White House? **Camille Paglia,** on Salon.com, 8 January 2008

She is a brittle, relentless manipulator

Colleagues ... the kind

of office people who like to pin up amusing headlines by your terminal are invariably also the kind of office people who remember everyone's birthdays and bring in little bloody cakes, invent pointless unfunny nicknames, download film-theme ring-tones from films called things like *Grinding Teeth*, *Vaulting Stress* and cannot pass you in the corridor without wittily pretending to pull a gun. (As opposed of course to the kind of people who are simply sulky misanthropes determined that no one shall have any fun, ever, unless they themselves are the centre of attention ...) **Euan Ferguson,** in the *Observer,* 15 February 2004

Communists Bing! Badabing! They're snuffing it! Bloated!

By God's guts ... 487 million! Of impalified cossack-ologists! Quid? Quid? Quod? In all the chancres of Slavonia! Quid! From the Slavigothic Baltic to the White Black Highseas? Quam? The Balkans? Slimy, Rotten as cucumbers! ... Stinking shitspreaders! Of ratshit! I don't give a flying fart! ... I don't give a fuck! I'm out of here, bigtime! Cow pats! Immensely! Volgaronov! … Tataronesque Mushymongoloids! … Stakhanovicious! Arselikoff! Four hundred thousand versts … of shitcrusted steppe, of Zebis-Laridon hides! … I've come across the mother of all Vesuviuses here! Floods! … fungus-infected arsewipes … The Tsar's chamberpots for you and your filthy perverted arseholes! Stabilin! Voroshitsky! Limpodick leftovers … TransBeria! … **Louis-Ferdinand Céline**, pro-Nazi French writer, lets off steam during the German invasion of the Soviet Union in 1941

Pathological exhibits … human scum … paranoics, degenerates, morons, bludgers … pack of dingos … industrial outlaws and political lepers … ratbags. If these people went to Russia, Stalin wouldn't even use them for manure. **Arthur Calwell**, Australian politician

The whole idea is to kill the bastards

Restraint? Why are you so concerned with saving their lives? The whole idea is to kill the bastards. At the end of the war if there are two Americans and one Russian alive, we win. **General Thomas S. Power**, head of US Strategic Air Command (1957-64)

Simon Cowell

Simon is so vain that if he went to a funeral he'd want to be the corpse. Unnamed 'rival in the music business' on the music producer and talent-show judge, quoted in **Hermione Eyre** and **William Donaldson**, *The Dictionary of National Celebrity* (2005)

Those Giles Coren e-mails

The journalist, reviewer and restaurant critic Giles Coren is known for his intemperate emails to sub-editors who have tinkered with his prose. The following (the first dating from 2002, the second from 2008) have been edited.

To: the Times subeditors
From: Coren, Giles

The quick brown fox jumps over the lazy dog. How fucking difficult is that? It's the sentence that bestrides the fucking book I reviewed for you. It is the sentence I wrote first in my fucking review. It is 35 fucking letters long, which is why I wrote that it was. And so some useless cunt subeditor decides to change it to 'jumps over A lazy dog'. Can you fucking count? Can you see that that makes it a 33-letter sentence? So it looks as if I can't count, and the cunting author of the book, poor Mr Dunn, cannot count. The whole bastard book turns on the sentence being as I fucking wrote it. And that it is exactly 33 letters long. Why do you meddle. What do you think you achieve with that kind of dumb-witted smart-arsery? why do you change things you do not understand without consulting. Why do you believe you know best when you know fuck all. Jack shit.

That is as bad as editing can be. Fuck, I hope you're proud. It will be small relief for the author that nobody reads your poxy magazine.

You know fuck all. Jack shit

Never ever ask me to write something for you. And don't pay me.
I'd rather take £400 quid for assassinating a crack whore's only
child in a revenge killing for a busted drug deal – my integrity would
be less compromised.

Jesus fucking wept I don't know what else to say.

To: the Times subeditors
From: Coren, Giles

Chaps,

I am mightily pissed off … I don't really like people tinkering with
my copy for the sake of tinkering. I do not enjoy the suggestion that
you have a better ear or eye for how I want my words to read than
I do … It was the final sentence. Final sentences are very, very
important. A piece builds to them, they are the little jingle that the
reader takes with him into the weekend.

I wrote: 'I can't think of a nicer place to sit this spring over a glass of
rosé and watch the boys and girls in the street outside smiling gaily
to each other, and wondering where to go for a nosh.'

It appeared as: 'I can't think of a nicer
place to sit this spring over a glass of
rosé and watch the boys and girls
in the street outside smiling gaily to
each other, and wondering where to
go for nosh.'

*Dumbest,
deafest,
shittest
of all …*

Those Giles Coren e-mails (continued)

There is no length issue. This is someone thinking, 'I'll just remove this indefinite article because Coren is an illiterate cunt and I know best.' Well, you fucking don't. This was shit, shit subediting for three reasons.

1) 'Nosh', as I'm sure you fluent Yiddish speakers know, is a noun formed from a bastardization of the German 'naschen'. It is a verb, and can be construed into two distinct nouns. One, 'nosh' means simply 'food'. You have decided that this is what I meant and removed the 'a'. I am insulted enough that you think you have a better ear for English than me. But a better ear for Yiddish? I doubt it. Because the other noun, 'nosh', means 'a session of eating' …

2) I will now explain why your error is even more shit than it looks. You see, I was making a joke. I do that sometimes. I have set up the street as 'sexually charged'. I have described the shenanigans across the road at G.A.Y. I have used the word 'gaily' as a gentle nudge. And 'looking for a nosh' has a secondary meaning of looking for a blowjob. Not specifically gay, for this is Soho, and there are plenty of girls there who take money for noshing boys. 'Looking for nosh' does not have that ambiguity. The joke is gone. I only wrote that sodding paragraph to make that joke. And you've

> *I am sorry if this looks petty, but …*

fucking stripped it out like a pissed Irish plasterer restoring a renaissance fresco and thinking Jesus looks shit with a beard so plastering over it. You might as well have removed the whole paragraph. I mean, fucking Christ, don't you read the copy?

3) And worst of all. Dumbest, deafest, shittest of all, you have removed the unstressed 'a' so that the stress that should have fallen on 'nosh' is lost, and my piece ends on an unstressed syllable. When you're winding up a piece of prose, metre is crucial. Can't you hear? Can't you hear that it is wrong? It's not fucking rocket science. It's fucking pre-GCSE scansion. I have written 350 restaurant reviews for The Times and I have never ended on an

Fuck, fuck, fuck, fuck

unstressed syllable. Fuck, fuck, fuck, fuck. I am sorry if this looks petty (last time I mailed a Times sub about the change of a single word I got in all sorts of trouble) but I care deeply about my work and I hate to have it fucked up by shit subbing … And, just out of interest, I'd like whoever made that change to email me and tell me why. Tell me the exact reasoning which led you to remove that word from my copy. Right, Sorry to go on. Anger, real steaming fucking anger, can make a man verbose.

All the best

Giles

Cricket and Cricketers   A poof's game.   Kevin McCarra,

Scottish football writer, in the *Guardian*, 25 August 2005

Those who run cricket in this country, especially at the domestic level, are for the most part a self-serving, pusillanimous and self-important bunch of myopic dinosaurs.   Henry Blofeld, in the *Independent*

Cricketer: a creature very nearly as stupid as a dog.   Bernard Levin, in *The Times*, 1965

After a vote to admit women to the 211-year old Marylebone Cricket Club:
They might as well bulldoze Lord's. I'll never go there again.
Anon. MCC member

Critics   Critics are a dissembling, dishonest, contemptible race of men. Asking a working writer what he thinks about critics is like asking a lamppost what it feels about dogs.   John Osborne

Drooling, drivelling, doleful, depressing, dropsical drips.
Sir Thomas Beecham

Of the New York critics Frank Rich and John Simon:
The syphilis and gonorrhoea of the theatre.   David Mamet, US playwright

Donkeyosities, egotistical earthworms, hog-washing hooligans, critic cads, random hacks of illiteration, talent wipers of wormy order, the gas-bag section, poking hounds, poisonous apes, maggoty numbskulls, evil-minded snapshots of spleen and, worst of all, the mushroom class of idiotic.   Amanda McKittrick Ros (1860–1939), Irish novelist celebrated for the awfulness of her prose.

A Gentleman's Game?

As the young Geoffrey Boycott walked out to bat for England at Trent Bridge:
Hey Garth, look at this four-eyed fucker. He can't fucking bat, knock those fucking glasses off him straight away. **Bobby Simpson**, Australian captain, to the fast bowler 'Garth' MacKenzie, 1964

What do you think this is, a fucking tea party?

Advice to Boycott when he was scoring slowly for Yorkshire during the 1965 Gillette Cup final:
Next bloody ball, bloody belt it, or I'll wrap your bat around your bloody head. Yorkshire batsman **Brian Close**

When England's Robin Smith asked for a glass of water during a Test match:
What do you think this is, a fucking tea party? No, you can't have a fucking glass of water. You can fucking wait like the rest of us. Australian captain **Allan Border**, 1989

When Australian fast bowler Craig McDermott asked his captain, Allan Border, if he could change ends during a match at Taunton:
Hey, hey, hey, hey! I'm fucking talking to you. Come here, come here, come here, come here … Do that again and you're on the next plane home, son … What was that? You fucking test me and you'll see. **Allan Border** during Australia's 1993 Ashes tour of England; quoted on cricinfo.com

When Sri Lanka's rotund captain Arjuna Ranatunga complained of a sprain and requested a runner during a Test match:
You don't get a runner for being an overweight, unfit, fat twat. **Ian Healy**, Australian wicketkeeper

The Captain and the Umpire: Mike Gatting vs Shakoor Rana

During a test match in Faisalabad, 1987, the England captain Mike Gatting gestured to one of his fielders to move as the bowler began his run-up – a perfectly legal action. However, Shakoor Rana, the Pakistani umpire, accused Gatting of being a: Fucking cheating cunt.

In response, Gatting gave as good as he got, and both men pointed and jabbed their fingers at each other in an aggressive fashion. The match was suspended until the following day, and Gatting was forced to produce a written apology.

Men have been killed for the sort of insults he threw at me

Prior to this, one of Rana's superiors at Lahore Railways telegrammed him:
Do not supervise the match unless Mike Gatting apologizes in writing. He has abused the whole Pakistani nation and I cannot bear it. I think he is not the son of a man. That is why his face is from a white monkey.

Pakistan Cricket Board president General Safdar Butt commented:
Mike Gatting used some very filthy language to the umpires, and, let me tell you, some less filthy words are bastard and son of a bitch, and so on. No-one has the right to abuse umpires.

Rana later recalled:
In Pakistan many men have been killed for the sort of insults he threw at me. He's lucky I didn't beat him and even more lucky no spectator came onto the field to assault him.

Twenty20 Cricket: The Stanford Affair

In June 2008 **Sir Allen Stanford**, a Texan billionaire, arrived by helicopter at Lord's to announce a series of $20 million Twenty20 matches between his Caribbean All-Stars XI and England. The phenomenon of Twenty20 cricket, and Stanford's role in its development, caused outrage in some cricket fans:

But wait! What has happened to your warm and cozy sports pages? Where are those match reports you were desperately seeking? The sports page looks kind of strange, doesn't it? Big and lurid headlines screaming out at you … The sordid Stanford saga is furiously unfolding in front of you and is occupying more and more newspaper acreage by the day … I, for one, resent this intrusion … I am being forced to wade through sewage now to get to the apple tree. I am forced to sit at the opera next to this obese, loud, belching, flatulent man who will proceed to eat his greasy burger and fries during the aria, while talking on his cell phone. The library I borrow my Rushdie and Roth from has been renovated and will now devote half its space to pornography.

Oh, you think I am over-reacting here? I am being

> *I am forced to sit at the opera next to this obese, loud, belching, flatulent man*

old fashioned, am I? Being a purist? Not willing to change with the times? Clinging on to an idyllic past in the face of an ever-changing fast society? With all due respect to you my friend, that is the biggest load of putrid faecal matter you can throw at me. Bollocks to you, I say. In fact, I say that all the above over-used and over-abused reactionary platitudes are cowardly alternatives to admitting that things have gone awry. It *has* hit the fan, splattered across the room and *is* dripping down the walls.

It has hit the fan, splattered across the room and is dripping down the walls

Cringing at the failure to keep Lord's off limits to helicopters of megalomaniac billionaires trying to make leery indecent proposals to the English cricket team is not being a purist … And clinging to an idyllic past? I have news for you my friend. I am trying to cling to the absolute present. I am only trying to cling to the drama on the field here. To the bare bones dramatic reality of bowlers pitted against batsmen. And over-reacting? You call a fervent desire to not see the very pulsing lifeline of the sport, the foundations of everything we want to remember, enjoy and hold dear to our hearts – and I am talking about the players, past and present here – being made to debase their images in this sordid drama over-reacting? **Sriram Dayanand**, 'Stop pissing in my coffee', posted on cricinfo.com, 3 October 2008. In February 2009 Stanford and three of his companies were charged with 'massive ongoing fraud'.

Tom Cruise   American film star This carbon copy of every other rich asshole … Extremely convincing when he plays an ambitious, superficial prick.   **The Beast's** '50 Most Loathsome People in America 2004'

Cyclists   Trespassers in the motorcar's domain, they do not pay road tax and therefore have no right to be on the road, some of them even believe they are going fast enough to not be an obstruction. Run them down to prove them wrong.   Jeremy Clarkson

Run them down to prove them wrong

A festive custom we could do worse than foster would be stringing piano wire across country lanes to decapitate cyclists. It's not just the Lycra, though Heaven knows this atrocity alone should be a capital offence; nor the helmets, though these ludicrous items of headgear are designed to protect the only part of a cyclist that is not usefully employed; nor the self-righteousness, though a small band of sports cyclists on winter's morning emits more of that than a cathedral at evensong; nor even the brutish disregard for all other road users, though the lynching of a cyclist by a mob of mothers with pushchairs would be a joy to witness.   **Matthew Parris**, 'What's smug and deserves to be decapitated?', in *The Times*, 27 December 2007. It turned out that Parris was objecting to the quantities of plastic bottles of high-energy drinks stuffed into country hedgerows at cyclist height. The article attracted 584 complaints to the Press Complaints Commission, making it the most complained-about article of 2007.

Does cycling turn you into an insolent jerk? Or are insolent jerks drawn disproportionately to cycling?   **Matthew Parris**, ending the same article

From
Dawkins
to
Dublin

Richard Dawkins Nothing returns one quicker
to God than the sight of a scientist with no imagination, no
vocabulary, no sympathy, no comprehension of metaphor and
no wit, looking soulless amid the wonders of nature. Novelist **Howard
Jacobson** on the scientist and evangelical atheist, in the *Independent*, 21 January 2006

Despair Caught in the grip of DESPAIR!? Times are tough,
eh, Bud? Nobody said it was going to be a bed of roses! So now
you've made your bed, so now EAT it! Or, you might say, you've
buttered your bread, now sleep in it! Who do you think YOU are?
GOD? What gives YOU the right to think you should have it any
better than the NEXT guy? Forget it! There's NO HOPE! That's
right, kids! NO HOPE! Face facts! Look at the world situation!
How long can you go on deluding yourself that things will get
better? The only thing to do is to resign yourself to the fatal
inevitability of it all! **Robert Crumb**, *Plunge into the Depths of Despair* (1970)

Princess Diana A harlot and a trollop. Words attributed to
Prince Philip. A Palace statement issued in November 2002 stated: 'Prince Philip wishes to
make it clear that at no point did he ever use the insulting terms described in media reports.'

A witless little girl unfit for marriage with
anyone … a destructive little chancer
emotionally located in the foothills of
adolescence … The facts: that she is
a virtuoso of on-camera tears, that
her delight in life is the nightclub
and that she seems to have no
mind at all … a frothball … **Edward
Pearce**, 'The Aspirin of the People', in the *Guardian*

*A witless
little girl …
a destructive
little chancer*

A sort of social hand-grenade, ready to explode, leaving unsuspecting playboys legless and broken. **Trevor Phillips**, just before her death

Had she lived, she would probably have ended up rattling around some draughty chateau, surrounded by autographed photos of Duran Duran, bemoaning to her faithful retainer Burrell that she was still big, it was the world which got small … The only paparazzi pictures still to get published would be those bitching about her cellulite as she was lowered into the Med from the yacht of some ageing Eurotrash playboy … You can just see her paying a visit to the climate change camp at Heathrow in the early hours of the morning, weeping crocodile tears over the fate of Eskimos allegedly threatened by putting on a few extra flights at Stansted. Either that, or she'd have turned up in the jungle on a special royal version of *I'm a Princess, Get Me Out of Here!* with Fergie and that ghastly Kent woman … **Richard Littlejohn**, in the *Mail Online*, 28 August 2007

Cameron Diaz American film star She looks like something that just punched out of a grave. Christ, if I saw this walking out of a building I wouldn't know whether to stab it in the brain or take it to my lab and study it.

IDon'tLikeYouInThatWay.com

Rancid leathery carcass of an antiques bore

David Dickinson

TV antiques pundit Rancid leathery carcass of an antiques bore. Turded around getting on everyone's nerves then turded off. **aerialtelly.co.uk**, on his appearance on *I'm a Celebrity Get Me Out of Here*

Celine Dion Canadian singer

She's French. Actually she's from Quebec, but that's the French wanker province, so it's just as bad. Canada would be a pretty cool country if not for Quebec. France sucks.net

Dogshit It is a true fact that every

time God makes a new pair of shoes, he makes a dog on a high-fibre diet. The more expensive your shoes are, your lovely shoes, the bigger and wetter the jobby that awaits them. Oh yeah, dogs are very discerning creatures, y'know. You're comparatively safe in flip-flops, they don't want to do it on any old rubbish I tell ya, but nothing opens a dog's bottom faster than a pair of hand-stitched Guccis, believe me … There I was looking at my reflection in the shop windows, thinking 'You juicy basket, you lucky sod.' New shoes, feeling very groovy, feeling very sexy, having a little fantasy, thinking 'Oh no, not all four Nolan sisters at once, please …' Then I meet the one with my name on it … **Ben Elton**, on *Saturday Live*, 1986

Drugs You see, I think drugs have done some good things for us. I really do. And if you don't believe drugs have done good things for us, do me a favour. Go home tonight. Take all your albums, all your tapes and all your CDs and burn them. 'Cause you know what, the musicians that made all that great music that's enhanced your lives throughout the years were *rrreal* fucking high on drugs. The Beatles were so fucking high they let Ringo sing a few tunes. **US satirist Bill Hicks**, from *Dangerous* (1990)

You wake up and you've invited eight people you hate to dinner ...

The worst drug is the one with the smiley face, Ecstasy. Any drug with a smiley face as a symbol has to be bad. It sounds like the most horrible drug I could ever imagine: You wake up and you've invited eight people you hate to dinner. Instead of having a hangover, you have to have eight horrible people sitting in your dining room. I'd rather have a hangover. **John Waters**, 1992

You got this thing on DVDs now, where they say DVD piracy funds the drug trade. Funds the drugs trade? I don't know about you, but I reckon if you can't make money out of heroin, you're gonna struggle in general. 'Oh, the problem with this crack cocaine is people can just take it or leave it – thank God we're still selling the Harry Potters!' **Frankie Boyle**

Dublin It's a big con job, we have sold the myth of Dublin as a sexy place incredibly well; because it's a dreary little dump most of the time. Try getting a pint at one in the morning and you'll find just how raving it actually is. **Roddy Doyle**

A depressive and largely dysfunctional metropolis, with high crime rate, all-permeating corruption, an unworkable transport system and one of Europe's worst-dressed street crowds. **Vitali Vitaliev**

A dreary little dump most of the time ...

From
Electorate
to
Europe

The Electorate I was elected by a bunch of fat, stupid, ugly old ladies that watch soap operas, play bingo, read tabloids and don't know the metric system. **Tom Alcieri**, Republican member of the New Hampshire state legislature

Drop dead, you little cretin. **President Nicolas Sarkozy** of France, after a man had refused to shake his hand, shouting, 'Don't touch me, you'll make me dirty.'

Ben Elton English comedian and writer I don't think there's such a thing as integrity or being a sell-out – I just think he's a wanker. **Amy Winehouse**, on *Never Mind the Buzzcocks*

Drop dead, you little cretin ...

Eminem White US rapper Misdeeds: Expecting people to care about his shitty childhood because he is white. Dissing his mama. Lifting weights after he got famous. Is the official voice of white teenage suburban boys. Has already worn out his shock value to the extent that his next album will have to include slurs against paraplegics and land-mine victims just to raise eyebrows … Aesthetic: Trailer-trash … with just a hint of Down's syndrome. *The Beast's* '50 Most Loathsome People in America 2002'

England and the English

England is a horrible place with horrible people, horrible food, horrible climate, horrible class system, horrible cities and horrible countryside. **Stephen Pile**, in the *Sunday Times*

God, what a hole, what witless crapulous people. **Philip Larkin**, letter to Robert Conquest, 24 July 1955

> *Their spunk is that watery it's a marvel they can breed*

One cannot trust people whose cuisine is so bad … The only thing they have ever done for European agriculture is mad cow disease … After Finland, it is the country with the worst food. **President Jacques Chirac** of France

Curse the blasted, jelly-boned swines, the slimy, the belly-wriggling invertebrates, the miserable sodding rotters, the flaming sods, the snivelling, dribbling, palsied, pulseless lot that make up England. They've got white of egg in their veins, and their spunk is that watery it's a marvel they can breed … Why, why, why, was

I born an Englishman! – my cursed, rotten-boned, pappy-hearted countrymen, why was I sent to *them*? **D.H. Lawrence**, letter to Edward Garnett, 3 July 1912, after a publisher had rejected *Sons and Lovers*

In terms of teen pregnancy, we are in the lead, and when it comes to fat, lazy, inert lard-arses, we are in the premiership! **Marcus Brigstocke**, on BBC 4's *The Late Edition*

Fat, lazy, inert lard-arses

England's not a bad country … It's just a mean, cold, ugly, divided, tired, clapped-out, post-imperial, post-industrial slag-heap covered in polystyrene hamburger cartons. **Margaret Drabble**, *A Natural Curiosity* (1989)

That's us: a nation of prim, mimsy, curtain-twitching, tut-tutting, balcony-peering, small-minded complainers to our local councils and writers of letters to newspapers about split infinitives. We deserve to forthwith go up in smoke. **Sam Leith**, 'A sneer of petty disapproval posing as law', telegraph.co.uk, 15 December 2008

Racial characteristics: cold-blooded queers with nasty complexions and terrible teeth who once conquered half the world but still haven't figured out central heating. They warm their beers and chill their baths and boil all their food. **P.J. O'Rourke**, 'Foreigners Around the World', in *National Lampoon*, 1976

Cold-blooded queers with nasty complexions and terrible teeth

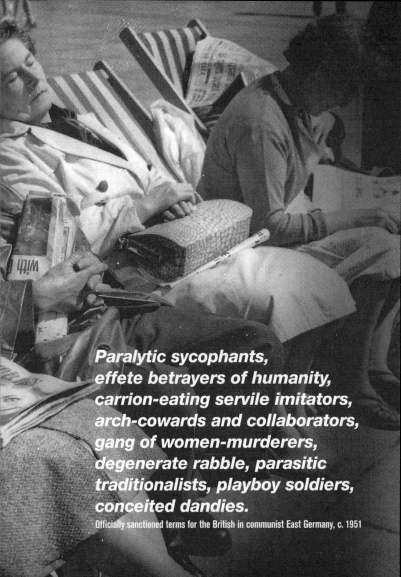

*Paralytic sycophants,
effete betrayers of humanity,
carrion-eating servile imitators,
arch-cowards and collaborators,
gang of women-murderers,
degenerate rabble, parasitic
traditionalists, playboy soldiers,
conceited dandies.*

Officially sanctioned terms for the British in communist East Germany, c. 1951

Damn you, England. You're rotting now, and quite soon you'll disappear. My hate will outrun you yet if only for a few seconds. I wish it could be eternal. **John Osborne**, letter to *Tribune*, August 1961

England has become a squalid, uncomfortable, ugly place … an intolerant, racist, homophobic, narrow-minded, authoritarian rat-hole run by vicious suburban-minded, materialistic philistines. **Hanif Kureishi**, in 1988, quoted in Patrick Higgins, ed., *A Queer Reader* (1993)

Look what these bastards have done to Wales. They've taken our coal, our water, our steel. They buy our houses and they only live in them for a fortnight every twelve months. What have they given us? Absolutely nothing. We've been exploited, raped, controlled and punished by the English – and that's who you are playing this afternoon. Welsh rugby captain **Phil Bennett** gives his team a pep talk before playing England, 1977

Estate Agents
Some of the people I hate most in the world are estate agents. I hate generalizations, but all estate agents are slimy, money-obsessed, lying idiots, who went to public school, but still didn't get any A-levels and so have to do an essentially unnecessary job for too much money. It's not a generalization. Show me one estate agent who isn't like that and I will show you an estate agent who has lied to you to convince you that he isn't like that and has thus confirmed just exactly how much he is like that in reality. **Richard Herring**, *Warming Up*, 17 February 2003, on richardherring.com

They will fuck you over at any given opportunity

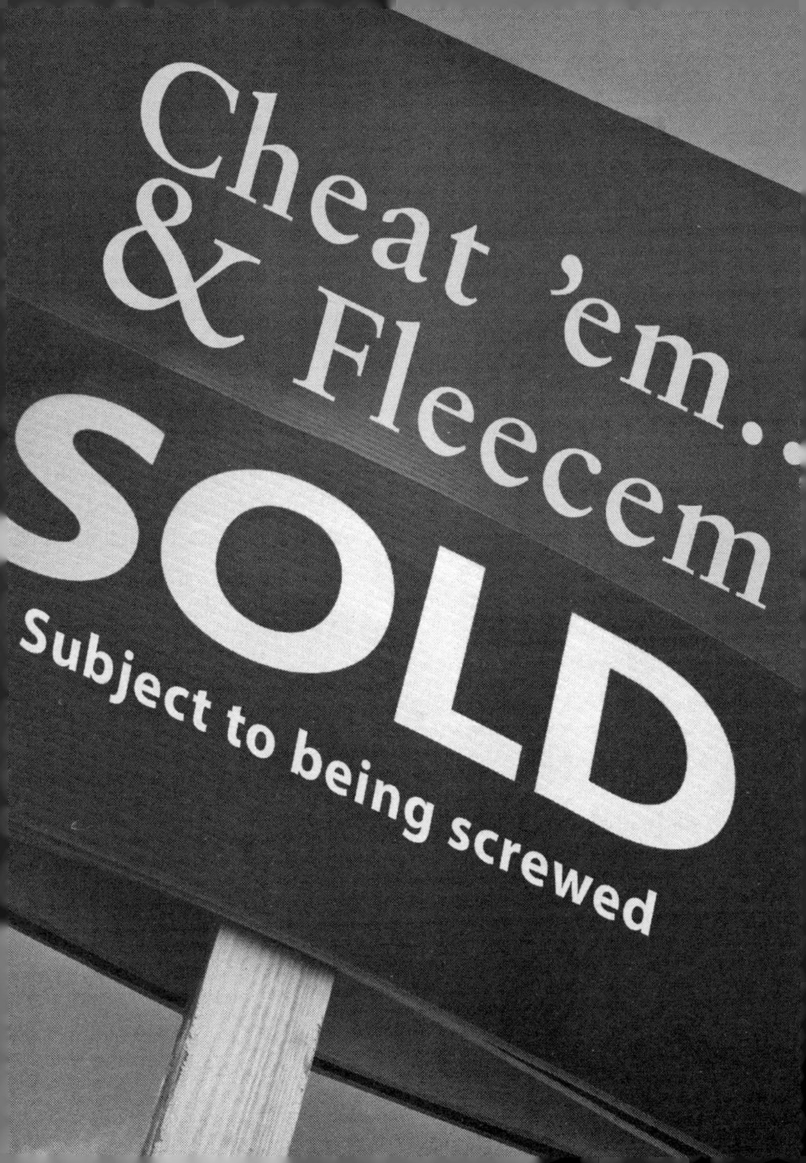
Cheat 'em...
& Fleecem
SOLD
Subject to being screwed

All estate agents are slimy, money-obsessed, lying idiots

I urge you, my friends, please be careful when dealing with these rodents, because they will fuck you over at any given opportunity … There's no real science or mystical theory to why estate agents are mentally inadequate. In fact, it's quite simple – the estate agent industry in the UK is unlicensed and unregulated, so any old fool off the street without qualifications or experience can set up shop … You have to ask yourself, what kind of person would actually want to be an estate agent? … The answer to that question is, 'a devious idiot that carries a joy for inflicting misery' … They all step off the production line in a cheap River Island suit, slicked hair, and a slimy personality that makes them think they're hot shit. Estate agents should be required to have a qualification other than that of a sharp suit. But they aren't. **Anon.** blog, 'Fifteen reasons why estate agents are idiots' 20 January 2007, propertyinvestmentproject.co.uk

I don't, as a rule, hate that many things. Hate requires far too much effort. What is the point of hating something when you can feel apathetic instead? I have work to do, bills to pay, people to see; I don't have the

I long to stick it up someone's arse sideways

time to hate. But sometimes, something comes along that is so easy to hate it would take more of an effort not to hate it, and that thing is Foxtons [the London estate agents] … I hate these people, but if I sell my flat through them they will obviously use aggression and tough tactics to get me the highest price, which would make me just as hateful as them. And you know, I am as hateful as them, partly because I am a journalist, but mostly because of the ease of which I have fallen into the trap of hating estate agents. Everyone hates estate agents. Even estate agents hate estate agents … **Bryony Gordon**, 'It's easy to hate estate agents, so here's how', telegraph.co.uk, 1 March 2009

Even estate agents hate estate agents

Did the agents care that a chain of desperate persons were cracking up, waiting, wondering, their hopes up and down on a big-dipper – it's on, it's off? No. They didn't give the tiniest toss, because for almost cocking up the whole chain of deals, producing a fairly crap leaflet and showing me round for 10 minutes, they earned £8,000, thank you very much. Plus VAT … Two days ago I instructed the hateful, mega-rich agents to remove their sign from the front of my new home AT ONCE. I refused to advertise their rotten outfit for one second longer. A young snotter assured me that it would be gone the next day … Their sign is still there. I am busting with such fury that I can barely laugh. I long to rip it from the gate-post, stamp into the agency and stick it up someone's arse sideways. Just another little dream of mine. **Michele Hanson**, 'I've moved. And I hate estate agents', in the *Guardian*, 26 June 2006

The European Union It's a German racket to take over the whole of Europe. You might as well give it to Hitler. It has to be thwarted. This rushed take-over by the Germans on the worst possible basis, with the French behaving like poodles to the Germans, is absolutely intolerable. **Nicholas Ridley**, interviewed in the *Spectator*, 14 July 1990. He later quit Thatcher's cabinet.

The French are a nation of collaborators … Germany's unique contribution to Europe has been to plunge it into two World Wars … French wine is mostly inferior to that of Australia but in their own rule-twisting way it's probably hard for the French to find that out for themselves … The purpose of the Government's European policy is to avoid being thrown into some bastardized, federalized, European destiny, actively and fawningly crawling to

Europe As Seen By The Yanks

No so much an axis of evil, more an arc of insufferability.
Unnamed US foreign policy expert

We're hot. We're on a roll. Check it out. We thumped Iraq. We whipped Communism. And now, at last, we put Europe in its place. US journalist on the Ryder Cup golf tournament held at Kiawah Island in 1991

Everything in Europe is lukewarm except the radiators … And the phones don't work. They go 'blat-blat' and 'neek-neek' and 'ugu-ugu-ugu'. No two dial tones are alike. The busy signal sounds as if the phone is ringing. And when the phone rings you think the dog farted. The Europeans can't figure out which side of the road to

France and Germany as the lesser countries insult us to the tune of their begging bowls … I wish I was not in the Community.
Patrick Nicholls, vice chairman of the Conservative Party, in the *Western Morning News*, 23 November 1994. He resigned the same day.

The real threat to peace and democracy in Europe comes from the European Union, not from Austria's pocket Führer, Jörg Haider.
Peter Hitchens, in the *Daily Express*

Britain does not wish to be ruled by a conglomerate in Europe which includes Third World nations such as the Greeks and Irish, nor for that matter the Italians and French, whose standards of political morality are not ours, and never will be. **Alfred Sherman**, adviser to Margaret Thatcher, in 1990

drive on, and I can't figure out how to flush their toilets. Do I push the knob or pull it or twist it or pump it? And I keep cracking my shins on that stupid bidet thing. (Memo to Europeans: Try washing your *whole* body; believe me, you'd smell better.)

Try washing your whole body …

Plus there are ruins everywhere. I've had it with these dopey little countries and all their poky borders. You can't swing a cat without sending it through customs. Everything's too small. The cars are too small. The beds are too small. The elevators are the size of broom closets. Even the languages are itty-bitty. Sometimes you need two or three just to get you through till lunch. **P.J. O'Rourke**, 1992

From
Facebook
to
France

Facebook.com May I make an invitation to anyone who wants me to be their Facebook friend. May I invite you to FUCK OFF … Facebook = just say no. **Arthur Smith, on arthursmith.co.uk**

Jerry Falwell

Right-wing American televangelist

On 13 September 2001, two days after 9/11, Falwell announced:

A little toad ... a conscious charlatan and bully and fraud

I really believe that the pagans and the abortionists and the feminists and the gays and the lesbians who are actively trying to make that an alternative lifestyle, the ACLU, People for the American Way — all of them who have tried to secularize America — I point the finger in their face and say 'You helped this happen.'

I think it's a pity there isn't a hell for him to go to. The empty life of this ugly little charlatan proves only one thing: that you can get away with the most extraordinary offenses to morality and to truth in this country if you'll just get yourself called Reverend. Who would, even at your network, have invited on such a little toad to tell us that the attacks of September 11th were the result of our sinfulness and were God's punishment if they hadn't got some kind of clerical qualification. People like that should be out in the street, shouting and hollering with a cardboard sign and selling pencils from a cup … I think he was a conscious charlatan and bully and fraud … If you gave Falwell an enema he could be buried in a matchbox. **Christopher Hitchens**, on Fox News, May 2007, after the death of Falwell

Fat Cats and City Slickers

How does something like this happen? How do people spend ten years buying and selling something with junk in the name, and then say, 'Oh, my God, you mean those weren't good investments? They sounded so *great*! Junk bonds. We thought we couldn't go wrong with a name like that. **Joe Bob Briggs**, US writer

Bankers … occupy a place in public opinion significantly lower than cannibalistic paedophile global-warming deniers. **Boris Johnson**, Mayor of London, 3 March 2009

What's the question most bank managers are asking these days? 'Do you want fries with that?' What's the difference between a bank manager and a pigeon? A pigeon can still put a deposit on a Ferrari. How do you get a banker out of a tree? Cut the rope. **Nick Curtis**, in the *Evening Standard*, 16 December 2008

Of Fred 'the Shred' Goodwin, disgraced former chief executive of the Royal Bank of Scotland:
He's a bad smell. He needs to be flushed away. **Joan Burnie**, in the *Daily Record*, 6 March 2009

How do you get a banker out of a tree? Cut the rope

After the troubled giant US insurance group AIG advised its employees to keep a low profile, following public anger that government bail-out money was being used to subsidize a reported hundreds of millions of dollars in bonuses to its senior staff:
Ah, it's a joyous day in Mudville when the pigs who've been raking in billions at our expense are so scared that they have to hide who they are, whom they work for, and what they do! … With all these thieving shitheads on the run, the good people at Connecticut Working Families are arranging a Saturday bus tour of AIG executives' homes … We at eXiled Online have already proposed a similar bus, but a much better bus, for AIG's executives. A bus that could take care of this problem cleanly, efficiently, and in an environmentally friendly manner. They're Chinese-made buses,

and they come equipped with lethal injection tables. We're pretty hopeful that tomorrow's bus ride is just a warm-up, and that the next time around, it'll be a fleet of Chinese-made 'Banker Recycling Vehicles' cruising Connecticut's billionaire-rows, pruning the population to save us a lot of tax dollars that would otherwise go to their future bonuses and pensions … **Mark Ames**, 'Class War for Idiots', eXiled Online, 20 March 2009

Even their girlfriends are awful

City boys are dicks, plain and simple. Look at them. Listen to them. Consider the carnage of the past ten years. What the hell were these idiots thinking? Even now they're still at it. In any sane world they'd all be herded into a shed and blasted with hoses until they promised to stop. Everything they say, think, do, watch, read and fill up their iPods with is awful. Even their girlfriends are awful. Straight women, reading this: if your partner is a City boy, leave him. Leave him now. Dump him with a text message, right this very second. It'll hurt for about six days, then your life will improve beyond measure. Sod that little number-swapping dick who dares call himself a man. Lob him in the shed with the other squeaking fakes and train the cold jets on the bastards. Shut the door and let them shiver. **Charlie Brooker**, in the *Guardian*, 1 June 2009

Fat People

Fat people are brilliant in bed. If I'm sitting on top of you, who's going to argue? **Jo Brand**

Don't let them be fat on aeroplanes or buses. Have No Fatties sections in restaurants and No Sweating sections on public transport and *Thank You For Not Wheezing And Puffing*

signs *everywhere*. Make it legal for employers to specify *No fat people need apply*. Make them stand outside in the rain if they want to be fat at work. **Michael Bywater**, Lost Worlds blog, 13 December 2006

Fatherhood
I'm a dad now. And I'm trying to do the right thing, you know, three or four o'clock in the morning, my wife's feeding our little baby and I'm going, 'Can I help you, love?' And she says, 'Clearly not, look at you, hmm? Curry and pies have given you many of the symptoms of the man-boob, but, as yet, the biriyani does not contain that magic ingredient that will allow you to lactate. Now piss off, you're scaring the child.' **Marcus Brigstocke**

Now piss off, you're scaring the child

Vanessa Feltz TV presenter Inclined to tell us a great deal more about her private life than we want to hear … Rumour has it that she applies her make-up in the morning by falling face down on her dressing-table; further that her underwear is stitched together by America's Cup sailmakers working double shifts.
Hermione Eyre and **William Donaldson**, The *Dictionary of National Celebrity* (2005)

Feminists A gang of muff-diving Druids. **Florence King**, 'the thinking man's redneck'

Let's get rid of Infirmary Feminism, with its bedlam of bellyachers, anorexics, bulimics, depressives, rape victims, and incest survivors. Feminism has become a catch-all vegetable drawer where bunches of clingy sob sisters can store their mouldy neuroses. **Camille Paglia**

Bullying, sanctimonious sermonizers

Women's studies is a jumble of vulgarians, bunglers, whiners, French faddicts, apparatchiks, doughface party-liners, pie-in-the-sky utopianists, and bullying, sanctimonious sermonizers. **Camille Paglia**

On equal-pay legislation:
An open invitation to any feminist, any harridan or any rattle-headed female with a chip on her bra strap to take action against her employers. **Tony Marlow**, former Conservative MP

Sir Alex Ferguson, countering journalists' questions about Juan Sebastián Verón:

He's a fucking great player and youse are all fucking idiots.

Quoted in the *Guardian*, 1 March 2005

Sir Alex Ferguson Manager of Manchester United

He's a bloody Scotsman, he shouldn't be part of any elite.

Ken Bates, one-time chairman of Chelsea, alluding to the suggestion that Ferguson was part of a New Labour elite, quoted in the *Evening Standard*, 16 March 2004

Football and Footballers Footballers are scum,

total scum. They're bigger scum than journalists. They don't know what honesty or loyalty is. They're the biggest scum who walk on this planet and if they weren't football players, most of them would be in prison, it's as simple as that. **Alan Sugar**, former chairman of Tottenham Hotspur, quoted in *The Times*, 15 February 2005

Football is so corrupt it's frightening. Until I became chairman I had no experience of the business at all. I couldn't believe what was going on. At the end of my first week the wife asked me how it had gone and I told her, 'If I get out of this without going to jail I'll consider it a rip-roaring success'. Unnamed chairman of a 'top-flight club', quoted by Harry Pearson in the *Guardian*, 20 January 2006

Footballers are scum, total scum

Near the end of another football season of spitting, punching, diving, cheating, roasting, bragging, assaulting, effing and blinding and various other sporting pastimes like financial skulduggery and forgetting to pee in bottles, can I make a suggestion? Next season can we make it an offence punishable by a long prison sentence to use the description 'The Beautiful Game'? **Michael Parkinson**, in the *Daily Telegraph*, 3 May 2004

Is anyone else out there bored to sobs by the ridiculous carry-on over the soccer World Cup? If so, please stand and join me. What a footling game it is, with its aimless to-ing and fro-ing and its nil-all draws and its narcissistic superstars collapsing in Hollywood histrionics at the merest whack on the shins. Who cares if Senegal beat Uruguay? Who gives a hoot if Becks does his hair in blond pigtails? As a listener told me the other day, soccer was devised to keep the drongos away from proper sports. **Mike Carlton**, in the *Sydney Morning Herald*, 29 June 2002

That Kevin Keegan 'I'd Love It' Rant

I will love it if we beat them, love it

When he was manager of Newcastle United during the 1995–6 season, Keegan, during a live television interview, launched the following broadside against his arch-rival Alex Ferguson, manager of Manchester United:

When you do that with footballers like he said about Leeds and when you do things like that about a man like Stuart Pearce – I, I, I've kept really quiet, but I'll tell you something, he went down in my estimation when he said that. We have not resorted to that, but I'll tell ya, you can tell him now, he'll be watching it, we're still fighting for this title, and he's got to go to Middlesbrough and get something, and, and I'll tell you, honestly, I will *love* it if we beat them, *love* it.

As it transpired, Man U's 3–0 victory at Middlesbrough secured them the title.

'Some of the Players Don't Deserve to Live'

In February 2003 Jesus Gil, former president and owner of Atletico Madrid, launched into a career-ending rant live on Spanish radio, attacking his own team:

They can stick my heart up their arses

There's too many passengers in the team. They're not going to laugh at the shirt any longer. Carreras, Santi and Otero are no good. They can die … I mean it, some of the players don't deserve to live … and anyone who doesn't like it can die.

When the presenter suggested he calm down a little (Gil had recently had coronary bypass surgery), Gil retorted:

'I'm sick of people telling me to relax. They can stick my heart up their arses.'

Pomaded hooligans forever being beaten up by bar bouncers and sleeping with common women.
Willie Donaldson, *I'm Leaving You Simon, You Disgust Me* (2003).

A pampered set of preening prats

A pampered set of preening prats.
Brian Appleyard, in the *Sunday Times*, 23 November 2003

Foodie Frets and Restaurant Rants

We were taken to a fast-food café where our order was fed into a computer. Our hamburger, made from the flesh of chemically impregnated cattle, had been broiled over counterfeit charcoal, placed between slices of artificially flavoured cardboard and served to us by recycled juvenile delinquents. **Jean-Michel Chapereau**, *Un Hiver Américain* (1975)

Of a burger from the Fine Burger Co. van at Lord's Cricket Ground:
It felt strangely cold, and hard. I pushed away the napkin and pressed the bun. Stone-cold. Fridge cold. Who keeps burger buns in the fridge? And the cheese looked as cold as a dead mouse on a foggy morning too: utterly unmelted, a rigid yellow edge at the corner of the bun … Inside the cold bun and cold cheese was a warmish beefburger …. The texture was stiff and mealy, the flavour grey, sad, doggy … This was not just a burger, this was a lavishly adjectived, preposterously over-described, linguistically inflated but nutritionally thoroughly bankrupt burger. It was an abomination, a horror, a downright summer food scandal. **Giles Coren**, in *The Times*, 30 May 2009

On a Lebanese restaurant in central London:
I wanted to grab ********'s manager and say, why are you doing this? The meatballs in piping microwaved yoghurt were an accident in a sheep-insemination laboratory. You plainly don't like running a restaurant; you take no pride in your product; you find the customers irksome and annoying;

> *The meatballs in piping microwaved yoghurt were an accident in a sheep-insemination laboratory*

you palm off unpleasant food to people you despise; and there's barely anyone here. Why on earth don't you do something else?
A.A. Gill, in the *Sunday Times*, 22 February 2009

It smelt stoutly of fatty, shredded incontinence pads

On an organic restaurant in West London:
I started with onion soup, which was straightforwardly disgusting. Tepid onion water, with a sodden Kleenex crouton. The Blonde had cod rillettes in a mason jar … It smelt stoutly of fatty, shredded incontinence pads, and came with two thin slices of bread that were so hard, Captain Bligh wouldn't have served them. 'You don't like the toast?' the waiter asked. This isn't toast. This isn't even a dog biscuit. The venison carpaccio … was covered in some concoction that made it taste like a medieval poultice for boils … **A.A. Gill**, in the *Sunday Times*, 15 March 2009

On the Ducasse franchise at the Dorchester, winner in 2009 of two Michelin stars:
… as sad as a funeral parlour, and with worse catering. An 18-carat stinker I wouldn't blow a raspberry at, let alone pin a star on. And it's gone and got not only two stars, but the turdy little indication that it can expect a third next year … It's all just so vacuously and incestuously French. So uptight and irrelevant and mincing. **Giles Coren**, in *The Times*, 21 February 2009. Coren goes on to describe the Michelin star-awarders as a 'ridiculous cabal of Gallophile fops'.

It's all just so vacuously and incestuously French

Gerald Ford 38th President of the USA Gerry Ford is so dumb
that he can't fart and chew gum at the same time … a nice guy,
but he played too much football with his helmet off … He's so
dumb he couldn't tip shit out of a boot if the instructions were
written on the heel. **Lyndon B. Johnson**, remarks on various occasions, 1960s

Foreigners Don't talk to me about Norway, and Holland,
and Sweden and all that rubbish. I'm talking about Royalty. Not
bloody cloth-cap kings riding about on bikes.
I mean, that's not Royalty. You'll never
see our Queen on a bike. She wouldn't
demean herself. **Johnny Speight**, *The Thoughts
of Chairman Alf (Alf Garnett's Little Blue Book)* (1973)

*You'll
never see
our Queen
on a bike*

If any of you have got an A-level, it
is because you have worked to get it.
Go to any other country and when
you have got an A-level, you have
bought it. **Michael Portillo**, speaking to students at
Southampton University in 1994, while chief secretary to the Treasury

I left a couple of my foreigners out last week and they started
talking in 'foreign'. I knew what they were saying: 'Blah, blah, blah,
le bastard manager, fucking useless bastard!' **Harry Redknapp**, in March
2004, while manager of Portsmouth FC

Formula One The point of Formula One is to export
lung cancer and emphysema to the impressionable youth of the
Far East and so long as it succeeds in that noble aim, the pressure
to be exciting is resistible. **Matthew Norman**, in the *Evening Standard*, 12 July 2004

4 x 4s The fat pink slobs who go roaring over the landscape in these over-sized over-priced over-advertised mechanical mastodons are people too lazy to walk, too ignorant to saddle a horse, too cheap and clumsy to paddle a canoe. Like cattle or sheep, they travel in herds, scared to death of going anywhere alone, and they leave their sign and spoor all over the back country: Coors beer cans, Styrofoam cups, plastic spoons, balls of Kleenex, wads of toilet paper, spent cartridge shells, crushed gopher snakes, smashed sagebrush, broken trees, dead chipmunks, wounded deer, eroded trails, bullet-riddled petroglyphs, spray-painted signatures, vandalized Indian ruins, fouled-up waterholes, polluted springs and smouldering campfires piled with incombustible tinfoil, filter tips, broken bottles. Etc. **Edward Abbey**, *Postcards from Ed* (2006)

Cheese-eating surrender monkeys

France and the French

A relatively small and eternally quarrelsome country in Western Europe, fountainhead of rationalist political manias, militarily impotent, historically inglorious during the past century, democratically bankrupt, Communist-infiltrated from top to bottom. **William F. Buckley, Jr.**

Cheese-eating surrender monkeys.
Groundsman Willie, in a 1995 episode of *The Simpsons*

Oh, please, don't tell me about the French ...

There's nothing funnier to me than the French. The French Resistance is probably the biggest mythical joke that ever existed. There were four guys in the French Resistance. They couldn't hand over the Jewish people fast enough. Oh, please, don't tell me about the French. The French have all sorts of secret deals with Saddam and everybody else for two cents a litre. **Jay Leno**, interviewed in *LA Weekly*, 16 September 2004

The only way the French are going in is if we tell them we found truffles in Iraq. **Jay Leno**

Why French People Suck:
Reason #1: Because they eat snails.
Reason #2: Because they eat horse.
Reason #3: Because they have dumb names like Jean De Du De Diddly Squa.
Reason #4: Because they are cheese-eating surrender monkeys.
Reason #5: Because we can nuke them bastards, and they can't do anything about it. **Brad**, North Carolina

You know why the French don't want to bomb Saddam Hussein? Because he hates America, he loves mistresses and wears a beret. He IS French, people. Conan O'Brien

I had a French girlfriend. It was like going to bed with a Rottweiler on your chest. And their breath smells as well. Gordon Ramsay, on *The Tonight Show With Jay Leno*, October 2007

France has a population of 54 million people, most of whom drink and smoke a great deal, drive like lunatics, are dangerously oversexed and have no concept of standing patiently in a line. The French people are generally gloomy, temperamental, proud, arrogant, aloof and undisciplined; those are their good points. Most French citizens are Roman Catholic, although you'd hardly guess it from their behaviour. Many people are Communists and topless sunbathing is common. Men sometimes have girls' names like Marie and they kiss each other when they hand out medals. American travellers are advised to travel in groups and to wear baseball caps and colourful pants for easier mutual recognition. All French women have little tits, and don't shave their armpits. France sucks.net

All French women have little tits, and don't shave their armpits

Who began the Panama Canal? *France*. Who finished it? *United States*. Who was defeated within moments of World War I starting? *France.* Who bailed them out? *United States.* Who was defeated within moments of World War II starting? *France.* Who bailed them out? *United States.* Who began Vietnam? *France.* Who tried to finish Vietnam? *United States.* France sucks.net

Gallic poncery of the worst kind

France has neither winter nor summer nor morals. Apart from these drawbacks it is a fine country. France has usually been governed by prostitutes. **Mark Twain**

On the French Open tennis championship:
Nothing in global sport is so metronomically mind-numbing as tennis on the Paris clay … Even now, there are black polo neck-clad men in the bars of the Left Bank, discussing the French Open as if it was some new proposition from Jacques Derrida. For me [it] … feels like Gallic poncery of the worst kind. **Matthew Norman**, *Evening Standard*, 24 May 2004.

Sigmund Freud   Austrian psychoanalyst Sigmund Freud was a half-baked Viennese quack. Our literature, culture, and the films of Woody Allen would be better today if Freud had never written a word. **Ian Shoales**, US humorist

I just want to make one brief statement about psychoanalysis: 'Fuck Dr Freud.' **Oscar Levant**

From
Gays
to
Guardianistas

Gays Homosexuality is a sickness, just as are baby-rape or wanting to become the head of General Motors. **Eldridge Cleaver**, 'Notes on a Native Son', from *Soul on Ice* (1968)

A man who lies with another man should be stoned. It helps, that's all I'm saying. **Frankie Boyle**

Germany and the Germans The 2012 London Olympics were supposed to restore British national pride. £20 billion to restore British national pride? For £20 billion, we could have written 'FUCK OFF GERMANY' on the moon. **Frankie Boyle**

Racial characteristics: piggish-looking sadomasochistic automatons whose only known forms of relaxation are swilling watery beer from vast tubs and singing the idiotically repetitive verses of their porcine folk tunes … Their language lacks any semblance of civilized speech. Their usual diet consists almost wholly of old cabbage and sections of animal intestines filled with blood and gore. **P.J. O'Rourke**, 'Foreigners Around the World', in *National Lampoon*, 1976

For £20 billion, we could have written 'FUCK OFF GERMANY' on the moon

The British motor industry is really owned by Nazis.
Jeremy Clarkson, in 1998

Of the German army, post-Hitler:
Marijuana smokers, drug addicts, long-hairs, homosexuals and unionists. **General Augusto Pinochet**, former dictator of Chile

Life is never so bad that Germany is better. Jeremy Clarkson

Serial ranter no. 3

Noel Gallagher

Foul-mouthed frontman of Britpop band Oasis

On himself:

This guy came up to me from some band and he said that 'Man, I'd hate to be you right now, no privacy at all' and I was thinking, 'Sure thing man, I have a fucking Rolls Royce, a million dollars in the bank, a fucking mansion and my own jet and you think you'd feel sorry for me? What are you? I'd hate to be you, broke as hell living on the dole.'

On his brother Liam:

If I lived in America, I would have blown his head off by now and completely regretted it. Since I live in England, though, I just give him a black eye or something every now and again. I don't hate him, but fuck me, he pisses me off sometimes.

On Blur and its frontman Damon Albarn:

People say we're the Rolling Stones and that Blur are the Beatles. We're the Stones *and* the Beatles. They're the fucking Monkees.

Parklife just goes to show what a pompous arse [Albarn] is.

> **We're the Stones and the Beatles. Blur are the fucking Monkees**

Noel Gallagher (continued)

If you've got the time to sit down and worry about American culture creeping into British society then I would get a proper fucking job, y'know. Other people are too busy trying to make a living.

What does he know about British culture? He knows nothing. He's from Colchester, he's a fucking student, he took A-level music. He knows nothing.

On pop singer Robbie Williams:
He's a fucking circus monkey.

On Williams's 2006 album *Rudebox*:
Fucking dog shit … even he knows just how bad his music has become.

He's a fucking circus monkey

On Kylie Minogue, pop singer:
Just a demonic little idiot …
She doesn't even have a good name.
It's a stupid name, Kylie, I just don't get it.

On Phil Collins, pop musician:
Phil Collins knows he can't say anything about me because I'm the fucking bollocks and that's the thing that does his head in, and the fact that he's bald.

On hip-hop:

What's masquerading itself as hip-hop-slash-R&B is fucking horrible … The disregard for women, stuff like that, I find it quite sickening. And the clothes they wear, and it's all about 'me, me, me', and 'I wanna fuck you up …' Give it a rest, you bunch of idiots. I despise hip-hop. Loathe it. Eminem is an idiot and I find 50 Cent the most distasteful character I have ever crossed in my life.

Eminem is an idiot and … 50 Cent the most distasteful character …

On Nirvana and its frontman Kurt Cobain, who committed suicide in 1994:

Nirvana had this song called 'I Hate Myself And I Want To Die', and I thought 'I'm not fucking having that. He's got everything I fucking want. He's in the most fucking critically acclaimed band in the world, he's got millions of dollars. Courtney Love, well he can have her, but he's got everything I want and he wants to fucking die? Fuck that, fuck the song and fuck him.

Of his team Manchester City:

I've had enough. As soon as I get home I'm gonna buy that club. I'm gonna walk in and say, 'You … fuck off; you … fuck off; you … fuck off; you … make me a cup of tea.'

Golf and Golfers If I had my way the social status of
professional golfers would be one notch below that of Nazi war
criminals. **Andy Lyons**, in *Melody Maker*, 1988

There is one thing in this world that is dumber than playing golf.
That is watching someone else play golf. What do you actually get
to see? Thirty-seven guys in polyester slacks squinting at the sun.
Doesn't that set your blood racing? **Peter Andrews**

If you want to take long walks, take long walks. If you want to hit
things with sticks, hit things with sticks. But there's no excuse for
combining the two and putting the results on television. Golf is
not so much a sport as an insult to lawns. **National Lampoon**, 1979

Greens The truth is, environmentalists are just not attractive.
They're not winning, engaging, amusing or empathetic. They are
ranty, repetitive, patronizing, demanding, deaf, weirdly bonkers
and smelly … The real killer thing is the schadenfreude: the
naked, transparent, hand-rubbing glee with which they pass on
every shame, sadness and terror. No disaster is too appalling or
imminent that the green movement can't caper and keen with
a messianic glee … The enormous, vicarious pleasure they get
from frightening folk makes them repellent, and they get all hurt
when we don't thank them for it. Nobody wants to trust a future
to a bunch of malcontents who plainly have so much of their
self-worth and cachet invested in it all going to hell in a recycled
handcart … Green campaigners are a larger part of the problem
than jumbo jets and cow farts, and if your children drown or die of
thirst or skin cancer, well, you can just blame George Monbiot for
being so crawlingly unattractive. **A.A. Gill**, in the *Sunday Times*, 10 May 2009

We want to annoy the fuckers ... The best thing we can do with environmentalists is shoot them. **Michael O'Leary**, head of RyanAir, quoted in the *Guardian*, 4 June 2009

Grumpy Old Men (and Women) These

whingers are just bored complacent rich people desperately trying to pretend there is some sort of hardship in their long, well-fed and easy lives. It's easier to moan than admitting that if there is something wrong with your life then it's probably YOUR fault. **Mike Webster**, on news.bbc.co.uk, January 2005

I don't know what is worse: old men moaning, or people moaning about old men moaning, or people moaning about moaners moaning about moaning ... **'Dan'**, on news.bbc.co.uk, January 2005

Guardianistas

Referring to a nurse called Caroline Petrie, who was suspended for offering to pray for one of her patients:

The NHS, like every single one of our institutions, long ago fell to the Guardianistas, who pursue their agenda with a deranged zeal. While they genuflect to Islam and 'respect' every oddball religion from paganism to devil-worship, they despise Britain's Judeo-Christian tradition and use every extent of their powers to crush it ... Just imagine how they would have reacted had Mrs Petrie been a Muslim offering to pray to Allah for a patient's recovery. Anyone who objected would be accused of a 'hate crime' and dumped in a skip at the back of the mortuary ... There's only one word to describe ... the tell-tale creeps trying to get a dedicated nurse such as Caroline Petrie sacked for dispensing a little Christian kindness. Sick. **Richard Littlejohn**, *Mail Online*, 3 February 2009

Isle of Man

There are a few places in the world that have managed to slip through a crack in the space-time continuum, or fallen off the back of the history lorry to lie amnesiac in the road to progress … What is weird about Man is that, even though its main industry is money (laundering, pressing, altering and mending), everyone you actually see is Benny from *Crossroads* or Benny in drag … This was a prison camp in the war, and it is still the last seriously draconian wee country left in western Europe … only reluctantly and recently have they been forced to give up public flogging and hunting homosexuals with dogs … The weather's foul, the food's medieval, it's covered in suicidal motorists and … folk who believe in fairies and whip each other. **A.A. Gill**, in *The Times*, 22 January 2006

> *Everyone you see is Benny from Crossroads or Benny in drag*

Liverpool A cancer on the face of England. **John McCririck**, racing commentator. After this remark he had to be given police protection at the 1990 Grand National.

We all know that Liverpool is a hellish, cold tip of a place populated by self-pitying scallies whose idea of a good time is weeing down a rolled-up copy of the *Echo* at a football match. **Michael Bywater**, in the *Independent*, 21 November 2004

A hellish, cold tip of a place

… a city which is already the world capital of self-pity. There are soapy politicians to make a pet of Liverpool, and Liverpool itself it always standing by to make a pet of itself. 'Why us? Why are we treated like animals?' To which the plain answer is that a good and sufficient minority of you behave like animals. **Edward Pearce**, in *The Times*, 23 April 1989

Liverpool is a handsome city with a tribal sense of community. A combination of economic misfortune … and an excessive predilection for welfarism have created a peculiar, and deeply unattractive, psyche among many Liverpudlians. They see themselves whenever possible as victims, and resent their victim status; yet at the same time they wallow in it. Part of this flawed psychological state is that they cannot accept that they might have made any contribution to their misfortunes, but seek rather to blame someone else for it, thereby deepening their sense of shared tribal grievance against the rest of society. **Boris Johnson**, in the *Spectator*, 16 October 2004. He was obliged by the Conservative Party leadership to visit Liverpool in person to tender an apology.

h@!

From
**Have a
Nice Day**
to
Huston

Have a Nice Day

What I hate about contemporary life is a deep, unimaginative contempt for human beings *disguised as friendly concern*. If it weren't for this fraud, this pretence of friendliness, I could tolerate it easier. I would much rather have people say, 'Look, you *shit*, line up there, we don't give a *fuck* about you and your mean bank account.' There's no reason to be uncomfortable just because these people want you to be uncomfortable. There's too little opposition to this.

Paul Fussell, US academic, 1987

> *Look, you shit ... we don't give a fuck about you and your mean bank account*

Ernest Hemingway

US author When his cock wouldn't stand up he blew his head off. He sold himself a line of bullshit and he bought it. **Germaine Greer**

Henry VIII

English monarch A pig, an ass, a dunghill, the spawn of an adder, a basilisk, a lying buffoon, a mad fool with a frothy mouth … a lubberly ass … a frantic madman. **Martin Luther**, 16th-century reformer

The Heritage Industry

You can't stray within 50 miles of Haworth sodding Parsonage without being assailed on all sides by Brontë bilge. The Branwell Tea Shoppe. The Helen Burns Sunbed Centre. Mr Rochester Opticians. Grace Poole Loft Conversions. What a load of Wuthering Shite. **Lucy Mangan**, in the *Guardian*, 5 May 2006

> *What a load of Wuthering Shite*

Paris Hilton US socialite Won't go away … Brainless,
her spinal cord defies physics, like an Indian rope trick …
Her continued success as a celebrity famous for nothing,
despite the eerie resemblance she bears to the inbred banjoist
from *Deliverance* and a lack of talent so profound that others
become duller as they approach her, indicates that something is
fundamentally wrong with humanity. **The Beast's** '50 Most Loathsome People
in America 2005'

Maybe deep down, Paris Hilton is a gracious woman with a
profound concern for starving children and impoverished peoples
… Maybe there's some deeper meaning to the way Paris spends
money like it grows on palm trees, and
maybe that odd pose she strikes
in every single photograph of
her ever taken regardless of
the occasion – hips forward,
body angled, chin pushed out,
bedroom-with-an-hourly-
rate eyes blazing – is the result
of a little-known medical
condition and not outrageous,
overwhelming vanity … Our
cultural obsession with a woman
whose claims to fame include having sex,
spending her parents' money, wearing an ornamental Chihuahua,
and saying 'that's hot' – well, it's akin to eating EZ Cheeze on an
armchair outfitted with a working toilet. **Brooke Tarnoff**, 'Why you should
hate Paris Hilton', ugo.com

> **Her … success
> … indicates
> something is
> … wrong with
> humanity**

Christopher Hitchens

On himself:

I wake up every day to a sensation of pervading disgust and annoyance. I probably ought to carry around some kind of thermometer or other instrument, to keep checking that I am not falling prey to premature curmudgeonhood. *Love, Poverty and War: Journeys and Essays* (2004)

Anyone who disagrees ... can pick a number, get in line and kiss my ass

My own opinion is enough for me, and I claim the right to have it defended against any consensus, any majority, anywhere, any place, any time. And anyone who disagrees with this can pick a number, get in line and kiss my ass. Arguing for the motion 'Freedom of Speech Includes the Freedom to Hate', at a debate at the University of Toronto, 15 November 2006

A drink-soaked former Trotskyist popinjay ... Your hands are shaking. You badly need another drink. **George Galloway** to Hitchens, May 2005

Ho Chi Minh

I didn't just screw Ho Chi Minh. I cut his pecker off. **President Lyndon B. Johnson**, in 1964

Angelica Huston US actress She has the face of an exhausted gnu, the voice of an unstrung tennis racket, and a figure of no describable shape. **John Simon**, US critic

Those Hitchens vs Galloway Debates

In the USA in September 2005, Respect MP George Galloway and ex-pat British journalist Christopher Hitchens staged a series of debates about the Iraq War. Both parties engaged in bucketloads of personal abuse.

Hitchens on Galloway:

Ba'athist, short-arse, sub-Leninist, East End carpetbagger ... The man's search for a tyrannical fatherland never ends! The Soviet Union's let him down, Albania's gone, the Red Army's out of Afghanistan and Czechoslovakia, the hunt persists! Saddam has been overthrown. On to the next ...

Galloway on Hitchens:

What Mr Hitchens has done is unique in natural history, the first ever metamorphosis from a butterfly into a slug. The one thing a slug does leave behind it is a trail of slime ... You have fallen out of the gutter and into the sewer ... Ready to fight to the last drop of other people's blood ... You start off being the liberal mouthpiece for one of the most reactionary governments this country has ever known and you end up a mouthpiece and apologist for these miserable malevolent incompetents who cannot even pick up the bodies of their own citizens in New Orleans ... You once wrote like an angel, but you're now working for the devil, and for this I damn you.

You have fallen out of the gutter and into the sewer

From
ID Cards
to
Italians

ID Cards The new ID cards, they won't stop your identity being stolen. It just means that when you do, you're fucked. Oh, I've left my wallet at the hotel, I'm going to need new eyeballs and a finger transplant. **Frankie Boyle**

Instant tea We've more convenience foods now: instant Instant Whip and of course Instant Tea – so much quicker. Just pour boiling water on Instant Tea. At last! An end to 'pouring boiling water onto a tea bag' misery. I must try and let go of my anger about the wasted years of tea bag drudgery behind me – oh, the time I could have saved! I could have learned languages, pottery – Oh leave it, Linda, it's gone, it's gone. I believe Marks and Spencer now market a cup of tea that's already been drunk for you – just a brown ring in a mug. **Linda Smith**

Ireland Ireland is a modern nation but it is modernized only recently and at the moment it is behaving rather like a lavatory attendant who has just won the lottery. **Terry Eagleton**

Among the countless blessings I thank God for, my failure to find a house in Ireland comes first … The peasants are malevolent. All their smiles are false as hell … No coal at all. Awful incompetence everywhere. No native capable of doing the simplest job. **Evelyn Waugh**, letter to Nancy Mitford, 1 May 1952

The peasants are malevolent. All their smiles are false as hell …

Stick It Up Your Bollocks: That Roy Keane vs Mick McCarthy Bust-Up

The volatile Keane was selected to play for the Republic of Ireland in the 2002 World Cup, but before the competition, in front of the whole squad, he launched into an attack on the Ireland manager, the Yorkshire-born Mick McCarthy. Various phrases have been recorded for posterity:

Who the fuck do you think you are, having meetings about me? You were a crap player and you are a crap manager. The only reason I have dealings with you is that somehow you are the manager of my country and you're not even Irish, you English cunt … Stick it up your bollocks.

The tirade went on for some ten minutes, and Keane brought up 'every incident and perceived slight' since 1992, without once repeating himself. In his diary McCarthy noted that he had 'never seen any human being act like this before, never mind a footballer. He is delirious … I am every expletive imaginable from c to w … I was a crap player. I am a crap manager. I am a crap coach, can't organize training. I can't make a decision. I can't get inside players' heads. I can't manage people, even though I have been managing him with kid gloves for six years now.' Keane was sent home.

Brian Clough, who had once managed Keane at Nottingham Forest, commented: Oh, I'd have sent him home all right. But I'd have shot him first.

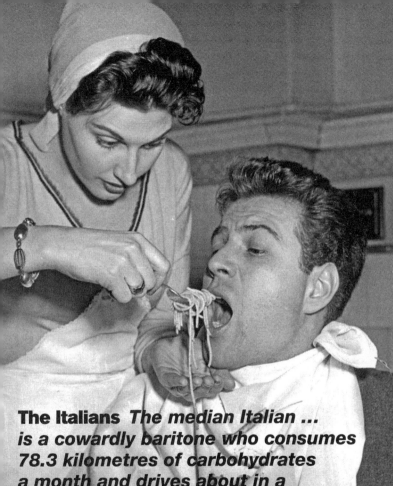

The Italians *The median Italian ... is a cowardly baritone who consumes 78.3 kilometres of carbohydrates a month and drives about in a car slightly smaller than he is, looking for a divorce.* Alan Coren, The Sanity Inspector (1974)

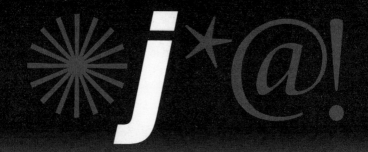

From
Jackson
to
Johnson

Michael Jackson US pop singer
With his womanly voice, stark white skin and Medusa hair, his gash of red lipstick, heavy eyeliner, almost non-existent nose and lopsided face, Jackson was making this appearance in order to scotch all rumours that he is not quite normal. **Craig Brown**, in the *Sunday Times*, 1993, on Jackson's appearance on Oprah

I respected him when he was proper artist before he started getting into all this cosmetic surgery shit. When he was in the Jackson Five, he was a genius.
Now he's just a fuckin' freak, man. **Noel Gallagher**

He hasn't just lost the plot, he's lost the whole fucking library! **Melody Maker**, on Jackson's 1992 concert at Wembley Stadium

Now he's just a fuckin' freak, man

Enough with the phoney platitudes. His incredible selfishness spending hundreds of millions of dollars on himself while singing We Are The World should make any clear-thinking American nauseous. **Bill O'Reilly**, US political commentator, quoted in the *Guardian*, 1 August 2009

Crimes: Surgically transforming himself into a ghastly artificial creature, and then forcing himself on little boys. His ability to remain at large and to find parents still willing to let their kids sleep over at Jackson's elaborate child trap both indicate a failure of our species as a whole. **The Beast's** '50 Most Loathsome People in America 2004'

Reviewing Jackson's *Moonwalker*:

Believe it or not, there was an age when Michael Jackson was a God. His songs were smash hits, his dancing was beyond compare and women fainted at just the sight of him rather than fainting at just the sight of him ... So we see the world's first universal answer to every joke ever written: Michael Jackson. We catch him at that stage where he wasn't really a good-looking black man anymore, but at least he was a half-way decent-looking white woman ... Wow, he's just ... so humble about his fame! It's like he doesn't even KNOW that he's famous! Oh Michael, please, don't be so modest! Indulge yourself a bit! I don't think the image of you as a shining, golden messiah is strong enough! Don't you have any oceans of water to walk on, or dead people to resurrect? I mean come on, splurge a little! **The Nostalgia Critic**, internet character created by Doug Walker

At least he was a half-way decent-looking white woman

Mick Jagger   Lead singer of the Rolling Stones   About as sexy as a pissing toad. **Truman Capote**

The Japanese   When it comes to Japanese civilization, it's mostly eyewash. Kabuki theatre is only just preferable to root-canal work. The three-stringed guitar is a sad waste of cat ... The samurai were thugs in frocks with stupid haircuts, and haiku poems are limericks that don't make you laugh ... If you asked

Japan is a lunatic asylum built on a hideous history, vile philosophy and straitjacket culture

a Japanese man to do something spontaneous, he'd have to check his palm pilot first … Japan is a lunatic asylum built on a hideous history, vile philosophy and straitjacket culture … Sex is where the weirdness of the Japanese peaks. I should start by saying that the widely held belief that you can buy soiled schoolgirls' knickers from vending machines is apocryphal, but it certainly could be true. It would hardly be out of character … If Freud had lived in Tokyo, we'd never have got analysis. He wouldn't have known where to start … **A.A.Gill**, 'Mad in Japan', in the *Sunday Times Magazine*, 2001

Ants … little yellow men who sit up all night thinking how to screw us. **Edith Cresson**, French prime minister, in 1991

Jogging Joggers are basically neurotic, bony, smug types who could bore the paint off a DC-10. It is a scientifically proven fact that having to sit through a three-minute conversation between two joggers will cause your IQ to drop 13 points.
Rick Reilly, in *Sports Illustrated*, 1992

I really hate people who go on an airplane in jogging outfits

I don't mind exercise, but it's a private activity. Joggers should run in a wheel – like hamsters – because *I* don't want to look at them. And I really hate people who go on an airplane in jogging outfits. That's a major offence today, even bigger than Spandex bicycle pants. You see eighty-year-old women coming on the plane in jogging outfits for comfort. Well, *my* comfort – my mental comfort – is completely ruined when I see them coming . You're on an airplane, not in your bedroom, so please! **John Waters**, 1992

Keith Richards outlived Jim Fixx, the runner and health nut. The plot thickens. You remember Jim Fixx? This human cipher used to write books on jogging. Now, what do you fucking write about jogging? 'Right foot, left foot, faster, faster, oh hell, I dunno, go home, shower.' Pretty much covers the jogging experience, I do believe. Then this doofus goes out and has a heart attack and dies … while jogging. There is a God. 'Right foot, left foot, haemorrhage.' US satirist **Bill Hicks**. Jim Fixx died in 1984 at the age of 52, shortly after taking his daily run.

Jogging is for people who aren't intelligent enough to watch Breakfast TV. **Victoria Wood**, *Thingummy Doodah* (1991)

Angelina Jolie American actress Angelina Jolie: more powerful than Oprah. She is No. 1 on *The Celebrity 100*, a list of the world's most powerful celebrities. From *Forbes*: 'Jolie raked in $27 million in the past 12 months …' Gee, thanks Angelina. You're so good at making us regular women feel inadequate. Next she's going to tell us that her vagina is made of platinum and diamonds. It is probably like Archimedes' death ray down there. Careful Angelina. Sparkly lips sink ships. **'Michelle'**, on IDon'tLikeYouInThatWay.com

Jordan (Katie Price) Glamour model and reality TV celebrity … along with fellow reality stars Jade Goody and Jodie Marsh, she has became a bargain-basement heroine for girls of little imagination and even smaller aspiration. Why do millions idolize these tawdry women, these great She-Chavs of the culture gutter? Sadly, it seems to be the money … Together, Jordan, Jade and Jodie form an unholy trinity representing everything that is cheap and regrettable about modern celebrity … The only thing well-rounded thing about Katie Price are her implants … **Jan Moir**, in the *Daily Mail*, 15 May 2009

Why do millions idolize these tawdry women?

Elton John

British pop musician

After Frank Presland, Elton John's representative, had made a complaint about the *Daily Mirror* to the Press Complaints Commission, the *Mirror*'s editor, Piers Morgan, was inspired to pen the following:

Tantrums and tiaras, darlings? Stick them where the sun don't shine

I have just seen your submission to the Press Complaints Commission. For sheer, pathetic, childish, toys-out-of-the-pram crap, it's hard to beat. I think it's safe to say the *Mirror*'s previously excellent relationship with you and your client has just ended. I'm afraid my staff and I just don't have time to pander to your collectively juvenile whims. Tantrums and tiaras, darlings? Stick them where the sun don't shine. Feel free to send this to the PCC as well. In fact, I will. And hey Frank, why not go further and take this grave matter to the European Court of Human Rights? Nothing less will surely suffice for such gigantic egos.   Piers Morgan, letter to Frank Presland, July 2003. The PCC rejected the complaint.

After winning a libel case against the *Sun*, Elton John opined:
You can call me a fat, balding, talentless old queen who can't sing – but you can't tell lies about me.

Elton John Fans   You're all ugly fucking pigs!
Elton John, arriving dressed as Louis XIV at Taiwan airport, September 2004

Serial Ranter no. 4

Boris Johnson

Mayor of London and formar Tory MP

Here he is on the phone to Keith Vaz, chair of the House of Commons Home Affairs Select Committee (HASC), in February 2009:

So fucking angry that you have gone on TV saying that I will be recalled to HASC … You are using the HASC for party political purposes. I used to think that you were a straight guy. A man that you could do business with. This is fucking ridiculous … You have gone on television and connived to try and give the impression that I fucking tipped off David Cameron. You are trying to make me look like a fucking fool. I cannot believe that you have allowed the HASC to become a part of this. This is such fucking bullshit … I fucking warned you beforehand that I would not be very good on details … You have behaved in an unbelievably naked partisan way. Labour Party? Fucking smear tactics from the Labour Party … I answered all of the questions and just because I cannot remember one thing. This is shit … You have made a mountain out of a molehill … The key point that is not getting across – I didn't give any fucking information to Cameron …

Johnson has himself been ranted at:

You are a self-centred, pompous twit. Even your body language on TV is pathetic. Get out of public life. Go and do something in the private sector. **Paul Bigley**, brother of Kevin Bigley, the Liverpudlian hostage murdered in Iraq, quoted in the *Daily Telegraph*, 21 October 2004. In the *Spectator* Johnson had berated the people of Liverpool for wallowing 'whenever possible' in their 'victim status'.

*@k!

From
Kay
to
Kinnear

Vernon Kay
English TV presenter Just what the UK needs now – another loud mouthed talentless Lancastrian being jolly and funny and gurning at the camera every three seconds like some lobotomised redneck ... If it were a straight choice between being stuck in a lift with Vernon or slamming my genitals in a walk-in freezer door for a couple of days, I would personally queue up and pay a tout over the odds for tickets to the freezer door. Or as Vernon would pronounce it 'doo-urr'. **The Daily Spleen:** 'Utterly pointless celebrities', on daily-spleen.blogspot.com

Paul Keating
Labour Prime Minister of Australia, 1991–6

On John Howard, Liberal prime minister of Australia, 1996–2007, on various occasions: Wound up like a thousand-day clock ... a dead carcass swinging in the breeze ... brain-damaged ... a mangy maggot ... like a lizard on a rock – alive but looking dead.

To a Cabinet colleague:
Just because you swallowed a fucking dictionary when you were about 15 doesn't give you the right to pour a bucket of shit over the rest of us.

Like a lizard on a rock – alive but looking dead

Kids These Days
On the news that Barbie has introduced a range of stick-on tattoos:

Tattoos are common and if it leads girls to get one, they might regret it for the rest of their lives. It is dumbing right down – Barbie should be at the high end of fashion, not the chav end. Whatever will they bring out next? Drug-addict Barbie? Alcoholic Barbie? Mother-of-three **Colleen Pope**, 35, quoted in the *Daily Mail*, April 2009

Robert Kilroy-Silk   Labour MP turned daytime TV presenter turned
UKIP politician turned independent MEP   How scared does a nation of people
have to be to vote for that orange-faced, self-aggrandizing, ****-
*******, ******, *****-******* motherfucker, seriously? I'm a
peace-loving hippy at heart, committed to non-violence, but he
cannot die soon or violently enough. I'd like him to go in a freak
yachting accident. Really freak, not even at sea, you know?
Just crossing the road one day … Whoosh! Yacht falls out of
the sky. If he's out for a walk that day
with Antony Worrall Thompson,
I will retire, that's it. You can
read about me living out my
days in the home for fully
contented humans, laughing
and dancing in puddles of
my own piss. **Marcus Brigstocke**,
on *Planet Corduroy* DVD (2007)

> *He cannot die soon or violently enough*

**In response to Kilroy-Silk's claim that
the Arabs had contributed nothing to
society in the last 500 years:**
Shakespeare hasn't done much in 500 years either. What's your
contribution been, Robert? Say, in the last twenty years, when you
weren't doing your show. When you weren't doing that crap show,
what's your contribution been to society? [*Kilroy-Silk attempts to
interrupt him*] Shut the fuck up! **Paul Merton**, on *Have I Got News for You*,
30 April 2004

That Joe Kinnear Press Conference

On 3 October 2008 Joe Kinnear, then interim manager of Newcastle United FC, managed to swear no fewer than 52 times in an extended rant to journalists, whose reporting he took exception to. There follows a shortened version of the news conference.

Joe Kinnear: Which one is Simon Bird?

Bird (of the *Daily Mirror*): Me.

JK: You're a cunt.

Bird: Thank you.

JK: Which one is Hickman [Niall Hickman of the *Daily Express*]? You are out of order. Absolutely fucking out of order. If you do it again, I am telling you, you can fuck off and go to another ground. I will not come and stand for that fucking crap. No fucking way. Lies. Fuck, you're saying I turned up and they fucked off.

Bird: No Joe, have you read it, it doesn't actually say that. Have you read it?

JK: I've fucking read it, I've read it.

Bird: It doesn't say that. Have you read it?

JK: You are trying to fucking undermine my position already.

Bird: Have you read it? It doesn't say that. I knew you knew they were having a day off.

Fuck off. Fuck off. It's your last fucking chance

JK: Fuck off. Fuck off. It's your last fucking chance.

Bird: You read the copy? It doesn't say that you didn't know.

JK: What about the headline, you think that's a good headline?

That Joe Kinnear Press Conference (continued)

Bird: I didn't write the headline, you read the copy.

JK: You are negative bastards, the pair of you.

Bird: So if I get a new job next week would I take the first day off? No I wouldn't. If I get a new job should I call my boss and tell him I am taking the first day off?

JK: It is none of your fucking business. What the fuck are you going to do? You ain't got the balls to be a fucking manager. Fucking day off. Do I want your opinion? Do I have to listen to you?

Bird: No, you can listen to who you want.

JK: I had a 24-hour meeting with the entire staff.

Bird: Joe, you are only here six weeks, you could have done that on Sunday, or Saturday night.

JK: No, no, no. I didn't want to do it. I had some other things to do.

Bird: What? More important things?

JK: What are you? My personal secretary? Fuck off.

Bird: You could have done the meeting Saturday night or Sunday. You could have had them watching videos, you could have organized them.

JK: I was meeting the fucking chairman, the owner, everyone else. Talking about things.

Hickman: Joe, no one could believe that on your first day at your new club, the first team players were not in. No one could believe it in town. Your first day in the office.

JK: My first day was with the coaches. I made the decision that I wanted to get as much information out of them.

Hickman: But why Monday? No one could believe it.

JK: I'm not going to tell you anything. I don't understand where you are coming from. You're delighted that Newcastle are getting beat and are in the state they are? Delighted are you?

Joe Kinnear: *Which one is Simon Bird?*
Bird (of the *Daily Mirror*): *Me.*
JK: *You're a cunt.*
Bird: *Thank you.*

That Joe Kinnear Press Conference (continued)

Hickman: Certainly not. No one wants to see them get beaten, why would we?

JK: I have done it before. It is going to my fucking lawyers. So are about three others. If they can find something in it that is a court case it is going to court. I am not fucking about. I don't talk to fucking anybody. Everything I fucking say or do. It is raking up stories. You are fucking – so fucking slimy. You are raking up players that I got rid of, players that I had fallen out with. You are not asking Robbie Earle, because he is sensible. You are not asking Warren Barton. No. Because he is fucking sensible. Anyone who had played for me for ten years at any level, you will find some cunt that …

You are fucking – so fucking slimy

Journalist: How long is your contract for, Joe?

JK: None of your business

Bird: Well it is actually, because we cover the club. The club say you are here to the end of October, then you say six to eight games, which would take it to the end of November. We are trying to clarify these issues. We are getting no straight answers from anyone. How long are you here for? It is a dead simple question. And you don't know …

JK: I was told the length of contract. Then I was told that possibly the club could be sold in that time. That is as far as I know. That's it finished. I don't know anything else. But I have been ridiculed. He's trying to fucking hide, he's trying to do this or that …

Steve Brenner (of the *Sun*): We are all grown men and can come in here and sit around and talk about football, but coming in here and calling people cunt?

JK: Why? Because I am annoyed. I am not accepting that. If it is libellous, it is going to where I want it to go.

Press office: What has been said in here is off the record and doesn't go outside.

Journalist: Well, is that what Joe thinks?

JK: Write what you like. Makes no difference to me. Don't affect me I assure you. It'll be the last time I see you anyway. Won't affect me. See how we go at Everton and Chrissy can do it, someone else can do it. Don't trust any of youse. I will pick two local papers and speak to them and the rest can fuck off. I ain't coming up here to have the piss taken out of me. I have a million pages of crap that has been written about me. I am ridiculed for no reason. I am defenceless. I can't say nothing. I can't do nothing. Then half of you are trying to get into the players … and I am not going to tell you what the players think of you all. So you will think I have a split camp. It just doesn't stop.

Journalist: But it's only been a week!

JK: Exactly. It feels more like a year.

Journalist: It's early days for you to be like this.

JK: No, I'm clearing the air. And this is the last time I'm going to speak to you. You want to know why, I'm telling

I ain't coming up here to have the piss taken out of me

That Joe Kinnear Press Conference (continued)

you. This is the last time. You can do what you like.

Journalist: But this isn't going to do you or us any good.

JK: I'll speak to the supporters. I'm going to tell them what the story is. I'm going to tell them. I don't think they'll interpret it any different, I don't think they'll mix it up, I don't think they'll miss out things. I mean, one of them last week said to me – I was talking about in that press conference where you were there, I said something like 'Well that's a load of bollocks.'

Well that's a load of bollocks

Journalist: 'Bollocks to that' is what you said.

JK: 'Bollocks to that.' And what goes after that?

Journalist: That was it.

JK: No, it wasn't, no it wasn't. What was after it? I don't know if it was your paper, but what went after it?

Journalist: I don't know.

JK: It even had the cheek to say 'Bollocks to Newcastle'.

Journalist: I didn't write that.

JK: That was my first fucking day. What does that tell you? What does that tell you?

Journalist: Where was that? Which paper said that?

JK: I've got it. I can't remember. It was one of the Sundays, not a Saturday. It was a Sunday.

Journalist: But you didn't say that to the Sundays, you said that to us. That was during the Monday press conference.

JK: I've got it, I've got it. I'll bring it in and show it to you. Why would I want to say that? And why would you want to put something like that behind it?

Journalist: Are you saying that someone has reported you saying 'Bollocks to Newcastle?'

JK: Yes. Lovely.

Journalist: Today we'll print the absolute truth, that you think we're cunts, we can all fuck off and we're slimy. Is that fair enough?

JK: Do it. Fine. Fucking print it. Am I going to worry about it? Put in also that it'll be the last time I see you. Put that in as well. Good. Do it … You're not going to fuck me off or frighten me in any manner. Whatever you do, or whatever headlines you run, you're not going to embarrass me. I'm not going to stand for it. I've come up here for a simple chance to fucking prove myself. Just wait, wait and make a decision after whatever period of time you want to. That's fine. Until then, get off my back and let me get on with my job. That all I ask. Just do that. That's all I ask of you. Fucking hell …

Fucking print it. Am I going to worry about it?

Subsequently, the Football Association issued the following statement:

'The FA has received an apology from Kinnear for any offence that his comments may have caused. The FA has borne into consideration the specific context in which the comments were made and the fact that the comments were made in a closed forum. While he will not face any formal disciplinary action on this occasion, he has been advised that in the event of similar public comments, disciplinary proceedings may be brought against him.'

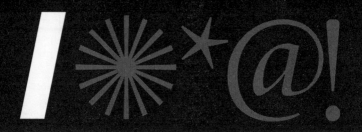

From
Law
to
Love

Jude Law English actor There's one face in the industry that is
guaranteed to make my teeth itch, my fists clench and the insane
little devil sitting on my shoulder whisper terrible things in my
ear. I'm sure you've heard of him; his name is Jude Law, and I
think I would prefer this planet if he was not on it. Ladies assure
me he is dashing, debonair and talented. All I see on screen is a
lanky streak of piss with a cocky streak a mile wide and a smile
that makes me wish for nuclear holocaust in his immediate
vicinity. 'Why I Hate Jude Law', on theshiznit.co.uk

Lawyers Lawyers? … they are evil. Most of them would
sell their mother into bondage for a few dollars … Most of them
are anal retentive … As a young adult, most lawyers make the
conscious decision that money is more important than having
fun … When it comes to social skills? They are a step above
mentally incapacitated … So why do I hate lawyers? Probably
because in addition to lacking basic social skills and being rude,
cold and bloodthirsty (those are the good qualities – I don't want
to get too nasty here), most of them also lack the one thing above
all that I prize in a human being … A decent sense of humour.
'MF', 'Why I Hate Lawyers', AssociatedContent.com, 9 January 2008

What's black and white and brown
and looks good on a lawyer?
A Doberman. **Mordechai Richler**

42 Reasons Why I Hate Lawyers …
(7) Because most lawyers are very
smart people who would have made
superb teachers, engineers, craftsmen,

They are a step above mentally incapacitated

A Judge's Rant

José Manuel Miguel Xavier Gonzales, in a few short weeks it will be spring. The snows of winter will flee away, and the ice will vanish, and the air will become soft and balmy. In short, José Manuel Miguel Xavier Gonzales, the annual miracle of the years will awaken and come to pass, but you won't be there. The rivulet will run its soaring course to the sea, the timid desert flowers will put forth their tender shoots, the glorious valleys of this imperial domain will blossom as the rose. Still, you won't be here to see. From every tree top some wild woods songster will carol his mating song, butterflies will sport in the sunshine, the busy bee will hum happy as it pursues its accustomed vocation, the gentle breeze will tease the tassels of the wild grasses, and all nature, José Manuel Miguel Xavier Gonzales, all will be glad, but you. You won't be here to enjoy it because I command the sheriff or some other officers of the county to lead you out to some remote spot, swing you by the neck from a knotting bough of some sturdy oak, and let you hang until you are dead. And then, José Manuel Miguel Xavier Gonzales, I further command that such officer or officers retire quickly from your dangling corpse, that vultures may descend from the heavens upon your filthy body until nothing shall remain but bare, bleached bones of a cold-blooded, copper-coloured, bloodthirsty, throat-cutting, chili-eating, sheep-herding, murdering son-of-a-bitch. Unnamed judge in a district court in the Territory of New Mexico, 1881

A cold-blooded, sheep-herding, murdering son-of-a-bitch

etc., had they only decided to be productive members of society. (8) Because there is no limit to the lies, deceit and character assassination that can be rationalized by a lawyer under the excuse of zealously representing a client's interests … (14) Because when a lawyer achieves success, it usually means that someone else got shafted. (15) Because most politicians come from the ranks of lawyers … (25) Because a lawyer in Illinois was found to have billed a divorce client for time spent having sex with her … (28) Because lawyers react like vampires to a crucifix whenever it's suggested their profession ought to be policed by outsiders … (35) Because … the best lawyers get hired by the worst criminals. (36) Because the legal profession regards such amorality as a lofty principle.

Jim Olsztynski, '42 Reasons Why I Hate Lawyers'

When a lawyer achieves success, it usually means that someone else got shafted

Have you ever asked yourself why everyone hates lawyers? We need lawyers in our civilization don't we? Heavens no, what makes you think we need them? They do not produce anything … All they do is raise the costs on health insurance, car insurance, home owner's insurance, small business insurance … But is this enough to hate them? Of course it is, but would you like some more reasons? Okay fine, lawyers have rendered our government ineffectual and most of the politicians are lawyers and they never do anything. Everything the government does is inefficient, want to guess why? Lawyers. Surely there are some redeeming qualities out there for lawyers? Nope, none I can think of. You see in my opinion … lawyers are a plague against humanity. Lance Winslow, 'Why Do People Hate Lawyers?', on EzineArticles.com

Leeds United FC *Gentlemen, I might as well tell you now. You lot may have won all the domestic honours there are and some of the European ones but, as far as I am concerned, the first thing you can do for me is to chuck all your medals*

and all your caps and all your pots and all your pans into the biggest fucking dustbin you can find, because you've never won any of them fairly. You've done it all by bloody cheating. Brian Clough to the Leeds United team, on the first day of his infamous 44-day spell as club manager, July 1974

Lego Everyone who has ever walked barefoot into his child's room late at night hates Lego. I think Mr Lego should be strung up from a scaffold made of his horrid little pockmarked arch-puncturing plastic cubes. **Tony Kornheiser**

Liberace Extravagant US entertainer and pianist He is the summit of sex, the pinnacle of masculine, feminine and neuter. Everything that he, she and it can ever want … this deadly, winking, sniggering, snuggling, chromium-plated, scent-impregnated, luminous, quivering, giggling, fruit-flavoured, mincing, ice-covered, heap of mother love … This appalling man … reeks of emetic language that can only make grown men long for a quiet corner, an aspidistra, a handkerchief and the

old heave-ho. Without doubt he is the biggest sentimental vomit of all time. Slobbering over his Mother, winking at his brother, and counting the cash at every second, this superb piece of calculating candyfloss has an answer for every situation. **William Connor** ('Cassandra') in the *Daily Mirror*, 1956. Liberace sued, won and, in his own words, 'cried all the way to the bank'.

> *The biggest sentimental vomit of all time*

The Liberal Democrats

The Lib Dems are not just empty. They are a void within a vacuum surrounded by a vast inanition. **Boris Johnson**, in the *Daily Telegraph*, 25 September 2003

Abraham Lincoln

16th President of the USA Filthy Story-Teller, Despot, Liar, Thief, Braggart, Buffoon, Usurper, Monster, Ignoramus Abe, Old Scoundrel, Perjurer, Robber, Swindler, Tyrant, Field-Butcher, Land-Pirate. *Harper's Weekly*

God damn your god damn old hellfired god damned soul to hell god damn you and god damn your god damned family's god damned hellfired god damned soul to hell and good damnation god damn them and god damn your god damned friends to hell.
Peter Muggins, a US citizen, in a letter to the president

> *God damn your god damn old hellfired god damned soul to hell*

Rush Limbaugh

Right-wing shock jock

On Democrats:

I'm going to tell you, what's good for al-Qaeda is good for the Democratic Party in this country today. 15 March 2004

On feminism:

We're not sexists, we're chauvinists — we're male chauvinist pigs, and we're happy to be because we think that's what men were destined to be. We think that's what women want. 15 April 2004

On Mikhail Gorbachev:

I heard that Gorbachev digs America. I'd be diggin' America too if I were raised a Commie and my only escape was vodka. 14 June 2004

On Nancy Pelosi, Democrat speaker of the House of Representatives:

She's got about as much respect as an iguana swimming around in your bathtub.

On liberals:

Liberal talk radio is nothing more than a pimple on the rear end of a pig. 19 May 2006

On the death of Kurt Cobain of Nirvana in 1994:

He was a worthless shred of human debris.

On the death of Jerry Garcia of the Grateful Dead in 1995:

Just another dead doper. And a dirt bag.

Littering I've advocated public hangings for a lot of things. Littering, for example. You hear people say, 'There's so much mess in the parks.' Well, the people who work in the park system don't go round with bushels of litter throwing it around. They don't say, 'OK, guys, here's a hundred pounds of chicken bones, let's throw 'em all over the parks.' People are slobs; they won't walk twenty feet to dump their trash in a can.

I advocated the hanging of litterers ...

So I advocated the hanging of litterers in the parks. Just leave the bodies up there for a week. Boy, did I hear from people. **Mike Royko**, US columnist, 1987

I took a train to Liverpool. They were having a festival of litter when I arrived. Citizens had taken time off from their busy activities to add crisp packets, empty cigarette boxes, and carrier bags to the otherwise bland and neglected landscape. They fluttered gaily in the bushes and brought colour and texture to pavements and gutters. And to think that elsewhere we stick these objects in rubbish bags. **Bill Bryson**, *Notes from a Small Island* (1995)

Serial Ranter no. 6

Ken Livingstone

Labour politician and former mayor of London

On the press:

What a squalid and irresponsible little profession it is. Nothing prepares you for how bad Fleet Street really is until it craps on you from a great height.

On George W. Bush:

George Bush is just about everything that is repellent in politics … You have got this super-patriotic hawk who was a coward when his country was actually involved in a war and has the most venal and corrupt administration since President Harding in the 20s. He is not a legitimate president … This really is a completely unsupportable government and I look forward to it being overthrown as much as I looked forward to Saddam Hussein being overthrown. Quoted in the *Evening Standard*, 8 May 2003

He is not a legitimate president …

On the Saudi Royal Family:

I just long for the day I wake up and find that the Saudi royal family are swinging from lampposts and that they've got a proper government that represents the people of Saudi Arabia. Quoted in the *Evening Standard*, 8 April 2004

On 4 x 4 drivers:

Complete idiots. Interviewed on GMTV, 23 May 2004

After a party on the evening of 8 February 2005 Livingstone was accosted by *Evening Standard* reporter Oliver Finegold:

Finegold: Mr Livingstone, Evening Standard. How did it –

Ken Livingstone: Oh, how awful for you.

Finegold: How did tonight go?

Livingstone: Have you thought of having treatment?

Finegold: How did tonight go?

Livingstone: Have you thought of having treatment?

Finegold: Was it a good party? What does it mean for you?

Livingstone: What did you do before? Were you a German war criminal?

Finegold: No, I'm Jewish. I wasn't a German war criminal.

Livingstone: Ah – right.

Finegold: I'm actually quite offended by that. So, how did tonight go?

Livingstone: Well you might be, but actually you are just like a concentration camp guard. You're just doing it 'cause you're paid to, aren't you?

Finegold: Great. I've you on record for that. So how did tonight go?

Livingstone: It's nothing to do with you because your paper is a load of scumbags.

Finegold: How did tonight go?

Livingstone: It's reactionary bigots –

Finegold: I'm a journalist. I'm doing my job.

Livingstone: – and who supported fascism.

Were you a German war criminal?

➲ page 168

Ken Livingstone (continued)

Finegold: I'm only asking for a simple comment. I'm only asking for a comment.

Livingstone: Well, work for a paper that isn't –

Finegold: I'm only asking for a comment.

Livingstone: – that had a record of supporting fascism.

Finegold: You've accused me …

On the *Daily Mail*:

You can't expect to work for the *Daily Mail* group and have the rest of society treat with you respect as a useful member of society, because you are not. Quoted in *Guardian Unlimited*, 13 December 2005

On the American ambassador, whose staff failed to pay the congestion charge:

It would actually be quite nice if the American ambassador in Britain could pay the charge that everybody else is paying and not actually try and skive out of it like some chiselling little crook. Quoted in *The Times*, 28 March 2006

On Metronet's role in maintaining and upgrading various parts of the London Underground:

They should be sacked, hung, drawn and quartered …

I think they should be sacked, hung, drawn and quartered, thrown out of the country and the whole thing returned to public ownership … They can go out and raise the money amongst their shareholders who came here to get their snout in the trough – they screwed it up; they are not getting any of our money. At a press conference, 13 March 2007

Love Love is two minutes fifty-two seconds of squishing noises. It shows your mind isn't clicking right. **Johnny Rotten**

Love ... a welter of self-induced miseries

Love, love, love – all the wretched cant of it, masking egotism, lust, masochism, fantasy under a mythology of sentimental postures, a welter of self-induced miseries and joys, blinding and masking the essential personalities in the frozen gestures of courtship, in the kissing and the dating and the desire, the compliments and the quarrels which vivify its barrenness. **Germaine Greer**

Romantic love is mental illness ... The second you meet someone that you're going to fall in love with you deliberately become a moron. You do this in order to fall in love, because it would be impossible to fall in love with any human being if you actually saw them for what they are. **Fran Lebowitz**, 1987

From
McCartney
to
Murray

Paul McCartney Ex-Beatle Has only produced manure
for the past 25 years. **Noel Gallagher**

John McCririck English horse-racing commentator An old
blusterer … a big spoilt kid, a pompous windbag … a moron …
a gargoyle. **Paddy Sheenan**, in the *Liverpool Echo*, April 2005

Opinionated right-wing bigot.
Wears his bigotry on his sleeve in
the hope that he will be thought
of as a lovable old curmudgeon.
He will, of course, be thought
of as the fat, sweaty turd he
is. **aerialtelly.co.uk**, reviewing *Celebrity Big
Brother* 2005

*The public
know what a
vile, hateful,
nasty piece
of work I am*

McCririck on McCririck:
I'm a nasty piece of work. I'm not
a pleasant chap, I don't have many friends. I bear grudges. I'm
malicious. I'm loathed in racing by jockeys, owners and trainers
… The public know what a vile, hateful, nasty piece of work I
am. Quoted in the *Guardian*, 16 June 2005

John Major Former Conservative prime minister John Major, Norman
Lamont – I wouldn't spit in their mouths if their teeth were on
fire. **Rodney Bickerstaffe**, trade-union leader, at the 1992 Labour Party Conference

A man from nowhere, going nowhere, heading for a well-merited
obscurity as fast as his mediocre talents can carry him. **Paul Johnson**,
in the *Spectator*, March 1993

Of John Major's government:
This is a government born in
treachery, surviving by subterfuge,
double-dealing and fraud, Janus-faced
and brazen, slippery and underhand, a
dismaying blend of incompetence and
low cunning, doomed to end in shame
and recrimination. I wish it the worst
possible ill-fortune in 1994 and trust that, come the summer, we
shall have seen the back of it. **Paul Johnson**, in the *Spectator*, 1993

A dismaying blend of incompetence and low cunning

Male Bonding
Can't anything be done about that klunky phrase *male bonding*? What kind of people invent phrases like *male bonding*? Can't anything be done about them, like cutting off their research grants or making them read Keats until they pick up a little respect for the felicitous phrase? **Russell Baker**

Manchester United
Cheating, whingeing scumbags.
Rory McGrath, on being asked what he thought of Man U, in *Total Sport*, 1997

Manchester United in Brazil? I hope they all get bloody diarrhoea. **Brian Clough**, after Man U withdrew from the FA Cup in 2000 to play in the World Club Championship

Peter Mandelson
New Labour eminence grise It was a strange day indeed when the stewardship of Keir Hardie's party [was] handed to Hyacinth Bucket for safe keeping. All those ponces that Mandelson mortgaged his soul to hang out with – the great and the good, they call them! But why? So far as I can see, the great and the good are in their graves, their bones turned to dust

and their party become a businessman's bunfight. **Julie Burchill** on the New Labour politician, in the *Guardian*, 9 January 1999

I was struck by the belief that this was the most arrogant, coldest and self-important individual I had ever laid eyes on. He made my skin crawl. Prince of Darkness? Master of the Black Arts? It is worse than that. There is no humanity in the man. There is no warmth. Mandelson seems to have complete contempt for his fellow human beings ... But if he is reptilian on camera, in the flesh he is repellent ... **Tony Parsons**, in the *Daily Mirror*, 26 July 2004

If he is reptilian on camera, in the flesh he is repellent

Barry Manilow
We live in a world where John Lennon was murdered, yet Barry Manilow continues to put out fucking albums. God-dammit! If you're gonna kill somebody, have some fucking taste. US satirist **Bill Hicks**, in *Dangerous* (1990)

Diego Maradona
Argentinian footballer

Gwaaaagghhhhhooooooool! Gwaaaagghhhhhooooooool! Gwaaaagghhhhhooooooool! Diegooooooooooooooo! Maradooooooooona! The greatest player of all time! ... From what planet did you come? ... Argentina two, England nil! Diegooooooool! Diegooooooool! Diego Armando Maradona! ... Thank you, God, for football ... for Maradona ... for these tears, for ... this ... Argentina two, England ... nil. **Victor Hugo Morales** greets Maradona's second (and only legal) goal in Argentina's World Cup quarter-final game against England, 1986

⊙ page 176

`Serial Ranter no. 7`
John McEnroe
Short-fused tennis star

You can't see as well as these fucking flowers – and they're fucking plastic. To a line judge at the 1980 US Open

You can't be serious, man. You can-*not* be serious! To the judge Edward James during a first-round match at Wimbledon, 1981

You guys are the absolute pits of the world! Vultures! Trash! To James again, in the same match

This guy is an incompetent fool. Complaining about James to the Wimbledon referee

You're a disgrace to mankind! To another Wimbledon judge during the same tournament

A bunch of stiffs who are 70 to 80 years old, telling you that you're acting like a jerk. On the members of the All England Club, after refusing to attend the Wimbledon champions' dinner in 1981

You effing son of an effing bitch, I'm going to effing do you and, if you report me, I'll effing do you again. To Centre Court judge Reg Lord, 2 July 1991. McEnroe was fined $10,000 as a result.

What other problems do you have, besides being unemployed, a moron and a dork? To a spectator

You got a fucking appointment to get to? What the fuck do you care, asshole? To a spectator who protested that play was being held up after McEnroe had challenged yet another call

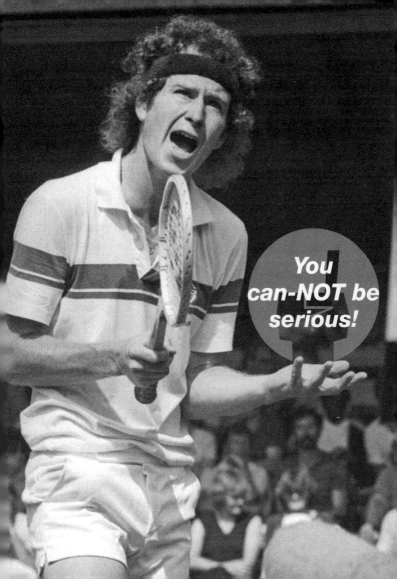

Maradona was ungracious in victory, and in his 2004 autobiography *El Diego* he had this to say about Peter Shilton, England's goalkeeper in 1986:

The Thermos-head got cross because of my hand goal. What about the other one, Shilton, didn't you see that one? He didn't invite me to his testimonial … oh, my heart bleeds! How many people go to a goalkeeper's testimonial anyway. A goalkeeper's!

Jodie Marsh Glamour model, WAG and TV celebrity Jodie Marsh, as far as I can tell, is a sort of sub-species of Jordan, but uglier and shallower. 'Jude 1', on Celebrity Hate Club, www.wereallneighbours.co.uk

A girl who has been on more laps than a curry-house napkin … Jan Moir, in the *Daily Mail*, 15 May 2009

The Media Run by idiots, lying charlatans and moronic twelve-year-olds who should've been drowned at birth in a bucket of raw sewage. **Ed Reardon**, hero of BBC Radio 4's *Ed Reardon's Week*, scripted by Christopher Douglas and Andrew Nickolds

Who are these unreconstructed wankers? **Tony Blair**, on the Scottish press, 1997

Who are these unreconstructed wankers?

Sir: … I have witnessed your decay from amiable drunk through voyeur and track rat to misogynous, vitriolic pariah … I cannot but from now on dismiss your scribbling as the libellous drivel of an unbalanced mind. Letter to the editor of the *Edmonton* (Alberta) *Sun*

The British media – they are all pricks. **Allan Border**, Australian cricketer, in 1993

On 29 December 2007, Prince Charles was taking a ride on a public road on the royal estate at Sandringham when he yelled at a photographer:

Get out of the way you annoying little prat. Can't anybody have a ride in peace?

An estate worker commented: 'Charles had spent the last five days with his family and there are bound to be some tensions when people are forced to spend so much time together.'

Get out of the way you annoying little prat

Where do they get these amateurs from? You're an amateur mate, go get on your bus, go home … Bugger off – get on your bus, you amateur … Oooh, I'm scared. Go ahead and put it in your paper. **John Prescott**, on being asked questions about Wales by a journalist from the *Western Mail* during the 2005 general election campaign

I think I'll just walk into the *Toronto Times* and machine-gun everybody. **Mel Gibson**, in 2001

David Mellor Tory minister turned football pundit

Of Mellor's affair with Antonia de Sancha:

Antonia de Sancha – always described as an 'unemployed actress'. Unemployed actress? How's she an unemployed actress? God, if you can feign sexual interest in David Mellor I should think Chekhov's a piece of piss. So she thinks, 'I'm an actress, it's a role. I'll prepare.' She gets to the bedroom situation. He's in a kit-off situation and there's Antonia giving it 'Red lorry, yellow lorry, Peter Piper picked a peck of pickled pepper.' But the hair, that's the main unattractive thing. What barber told him that suited him?

Someone winding him up there. 'Yes, David, that'll suit you mate, a greasy, oily flap of dirty-looking patent leather wafting about down one side of your mush – that'll drive those unemployed actresses mental!' **Linda Smith**, *Linda Live*, 1993

Men   Why are we shocked when 'ugly' women do things, rather than sitting at home weeping and wishing they were someone else. Men are allowed to be ugly and talented. Alan Sugar looks like a burst bag of flour. Gordon Ramsay has a dried-up riverbed for a face. Justin Lee Collins looks like Cousin It from the *Addams Family*. Graham Norton is a baboon in mascara. I could go on. But a woman has to have the bright, empty beauty of a toy – or get off the screen. **Tanya Gold**, in the *Guardian*, 16 April 2009, referring to the early success of singer Susan Boyle in *Britain's Got Talent*

They say men can never experience the pain of childbirth. They can – if you hit them in the goolies with a cricket bat for fourteen hours. **Jo Brand**

… the male is an incomplete female, a walking abortion … maleness is a deficiency disease and males are emotional cripples. The male is completely egocentric, trapped inside himself, incapable of empathizing or identifying with others, or love, friendship, affection of tenderness … He is a half-dead, unresponsive lump, incapable of giving or receiving pleasure or happiness; consequently, he is at best an utter bore, an inoffensive blob … To call

… hit them in the goolies with a cricket bat …

Every man, deep down, knows he's a worthless piece of shit

a man an animal is to flatter him; he's a machine, a walking dildo … he'll swim through a river of snot, wade nostril-deep through a mile of vomit, if he thinks there'll be a friendly pussy awaiting him … Every man, deep down, knows he's a worthless piece of shit. **Valerie Solanas**, *The SCUM Manifesto* (1968). (The acronym stands for the Society for Cutting Up Men.)

How do you know if it's time to wash the dishes and clean your house? Look inside your pants. If you find a penis in there, it's not time. **Jo Brand**

Men are still far too dominant for their own good, and consequently we've made a testosterone-sodden pig's ear of just about everything: politics, the economy, religion, the environment … you name it, it's in a gigantic man-wrought mess. The world's been one big dick-swinging contest, and we've caught our collective glans in a nearby desk fan … In truth … we're very, very simple. We're lazy and we like blowjobs. That's all there is to us. Literally: that's it. From Sir John Betjeman to Barack Obama, from Copernicus to Liam Gallagher. The core software we run on could fit in the memory of a digital watch circa 1985 without even scraping the sides. **Charlie Brooker**, in the *Guardian*, 1 June 2009

… flashers, grabbers, bottom-pinchers, purse-snatchers, kerb-crawlers, verbal abusers, peeping Toms and the ultimate cowards, the ones who roam in packs … **Valerie Grove**, in the *Evening Standard*

If we men had periods, we wouldn't have discreet tampon boxes, would we? No – we'd have boxes with MY FUCKING TAMPONS printed on the outside! **Ben Elton**

Sienna Miller English actress I once saw a 13-year-old girl give a subtler and more captivating performance as Celia in a school play. Limited to a gratingly narrow range of gestures and expressions, and the victim of inadequate direction and voice, the wooden Miller has to resort to the amateur's tactic – shout and exaggerate. She approaches an emotion with the finesse of someone beating a carpet. **Paul Taylor**, in the *Independent*, 23 June 2005, reviewing Miller's performance in *As You Like It* at Wyndham's Theatre

Princess Michael of Kent's Restaurant Rumpus

Seated next to a party of black diners at New Yorks's trendy Da Silvano restaurant in May 2004, the Princess – wife of the Queen's cousin – is said to have been annoyed by her neighbours' loud conversation and laughter, and allegedly slammed their table with the flat of her palm, saying:

Enough already! You need to quiet down.

They were stunned into silence, but as their conversation resumed, the Princess demanded a new table, and is reported to have pumped her fist and said:

Go back to the colonies.

When challenged over this remark, she said:

I did not say 'back to the colonies'. I said 'You should remember the colonies'. Back in the days of the colonies there were rules that were very good. You think about it. Just think about it.

The Princess subsequently denied she had uttered any racist remarks, and reportedly referred to her accusers as 'a group of rappers'.

Serial Ranter no. 8

Heather 'Motormouth' Mills

Former wife of Paul McCartney

Ms Mills – dubbed 'Mucca' by the tabloids, playing on McCartney's 'Macca' nickname – has long been the target of tabloid attention. In October 2007 Ms Mills waxed emotional on GMTV, in an interview with Fiona Phillips and Andrew Castle. In particular, she objected to her treatment by the tabloids.

Ms Mills: The press should have to reveal their made-up sources and their so-called friends unless it's a criminal situation, because they make up such lies. They've called me a whore, a gold-digger, a fantasist, a liar, the most unbelievably hurtful things, and I've stayed quiet for my daughter.

But my daughter – we've had death threats, I've been close to suicide. I'm so upset about this – I've had worse press than a paedophile or a murderer and I've done nothing but charity for 20 years. […]

GMTV: Listen, there will be people at home saying that at the beginning, Heather, you did use the press –

Ms Mills: I haven't used the press for anything except my charity. When did I promote a record? When did I act for anything? They always say 'publicity-seeker'. Look at me going to court. My pelvis is bust. You've seen the X-ray, right, which I had to produce because they put in here, 'Heather pulls her leg off', and, you know, talks about her pelvis. My pelvis has been broken for a while but I have

> **They've called me a whore, a gold-digger, a fantasist, a liar**

Heather 'Motormouth' Mills (continued)

months when I can walk and months when I can't. [...] It's fine that Paul can walk in going 'Are you all right?' and I'm hiding and I am the one that is abused daily. I have protected Paul for this long and I am trying to protect him but I am being pushed to the edge and I don't want my daughter when she is 12 going on the internet reading this totally one-sided story. I'm up to here with it. My plan is to change the law in the European Parliament and I will do it. And I'm fed up with the specific portion of the media. Some of them are still supportive but a specific portion are abusing me. I will investigate each and every one of those journalists. Everyone jumps on the bandwagon, makes money out of my misery.

Everyone jumps on the bandwagon, makes money out of my misery

GMTV: I know that, and I know you're upset and I know you're only human, which is what people are forgetting. But during the coverage of the divorce case they have been saying that you want £50 million.

Ms Mills: I have been offered nothing, OK, nothing. We go to court, nothing to do with that. We go to court over my daughter. I'm not allowed to talk about it because it's a criminal act if I talk about my daughter. You have no idea what's going on. These figures are made up – £100 million, £50 million, £20 million. How do you know if I even want any money? I'm £1.5 million in debt in lawyers' fees, and that's as much as I can say or I go to jail, for telling the truth. So I'm gagged at the moment because I'm not allowed to say a word while the media are fed this spin by a certain corner.

GMTV: One of the clauses, apparently, in this whole divorce thing, is that you want to be able to sell your story –

Ms Mills: It's rubbish. I can sell my story right now. I'm trying to protect Paul and our daughter. I am trying, and I'm being pushed to the edge. Eighteen months of abuse, 4,400 abusive articles. […] What did the paparazzi do to Diana? They chased her and they killed her.

Never mind all these other stories, that is what we are doing as a nation, buying these newspapers. Every time you buy one of those, you contribute to it. So force a change for responsible journalism. Rupert Murdoch, when he bought that newspaper, is quoted as saying 'I can't believe how easy it was to get in the British media. I can't believe it and I promise you I will always give you honest and straightforward journalism'. Nothing like it. And they will go for me tomorrow and they'll go she's crazy and she's this and she's that.

Go for it, because I will do even more. Sorry I got upset. I'm so up to here. Can you imagine being persecuted for that long. One of the guys, who I had convicted for assault – which they thought I wouldn't follow through to the end – had 132 convictions – 132 convictions and he's hired with no licence. They have to be licensed, because how do I know when someone's sitting outside my house if they're a stalker or not? It is living in a prison. The only respite I got was going to America, and I did *Dancing With*

What did the paparazzi do to Diana? They chased her and they killed her

Heather 'Motormouth' Mills (continued)

The Stars because our charity was so damaged that we needed the money. I was the only person on the show that gave the money to charity, and then they wanted to turn that into something awful – 'Get lost, Mucca', says the *Sun*. I've got 4,000 cuttings, like 'Mucca cha cha'. How do they mean 'Mucca' for doing glamour modelling, and they say it's hardcore porn!

How do they mean 'Mucca' for doing glamour modelling, and they say it's hardcore porn!

I would live in America in two seconds but I live here to keep my daughter close to her father. I compromise everything. You have no idea how much I have done to compromise. I have a box of evidence that's going to a certain person should anything happen to me, so if you top me off, it's still going to that person, and the truth will come out. There is so much fear from a certain party of the truth coming out that lots of things have been put out and done, so the police came round and said 'You have had serious death threats from an underground movement.' I was like 'Are you serious?' and they said 'Here's the 999 number', but I never rang the 999 number, I always rang the 0845 number. The press write I'm crying wolf for 999 calls, when the police came to me to tell me I had death threats and I had to be careful. That means my daughter's life is at risk, because she's with me all the time. Could I get security? No. Did I have to go to the bank and borrow it? Yes. It's disgusting, it's absolutely disgusting. Who created those death threats? The media. A certain part of the tabloid media created such a hate campaign against me, it put my life and my daughter's life at risk. That's why I considered killing myself, because I thought if I was dead, at least my daughter would be safe.

> *I thought if I was dead, at least my daughter would be safe*

And that is the truth, and I've got nothing to lose. I've got 300 friends who came to my daughter's party, and they are biting their tongues not to talk, because they're so loyal. Even a journalist said to my publicist, 'Her friends are so loyal, we can't even get them to say a word.' Whereas other people's so-called friends are putting stuff out right, left and centre. I just hope everybody goes on UK.com and starts taking responsibility for what we're going to feed our children for the next 20 years. We don't want them to live in a celebrity culture unless that celebrity is going to be used in life to make a difference in the finite amount of seconds we have left on the planet.

On 17 March 2008 the judge in the Mills–McCartney divorce case delivered his ruling, awarding Ms Mills £24.3 million, as against her claim for £125 million. While still in court Ms Mills poured a jug of water over the head of Fiona Shackleton, McCartney's solicitor, shouting:

> *I'm not a loser. You're a bitch! You're a traitor to your sex!*

I'm not a loser. You're a bitch! You're a traitor to your sex! How could you do this to another woman?

Liza Minnelli US singer and actress That turnip nose
overhanging a forward-gaping mouth and hastily retreating chin,
that bulbous cranium with eyes as big (and as inexpressive) as
saucers; those are the appurtenances of a clown – a funny clown,
not even a sad one … Miss Minnelli has only two things going
for her: a father and a mother who got there in the first place, and
tasteless reviewers and audiences who keep her there. **John Simon**,
drama critic of *New York* magazine

The above provoked the following anonymous letter to Simon:
You have obviously spent so much time with your head wedged
between your buttocks that your vision has been obscured by
the reflection of your own putrid entrails. If the art of literary or
dramatic criticism is to remain viable, we must seek to eliminate
people like you who degrade the art form by taking cheap shots
at performers' physical liabilities and who must darkly illuminate
their critiques with pseudo-intellectual name calling. If you must
insist in deriding Ms Minnelli's so-called imperfections, at least
do so with the stroke of your pen rather
than with the excrement of your bowels.

Modern Art [The British art
world is in] danger of disappearing
up its own arse … led by cultural
tsars such as the Tate's Sir Nicholas
Serota, who dominate the scene from
their crystal Kremlins. Most conceptual
art that I see now is pretentious, self-
indulgent, craftless tat that I wouldn't accept even as a gift … It is
the product of an over-indulged middle class (barely concealed

**Pretentious,
self-indulgent,
craftless tat**

behind mockney accents), bloated egos who patronize real people with fake understanding … It's a crime. We need art lovers to tell artists that they're not obliged to reinvent themselves into creators of piles of crap … **Ivan Massow**, in the *New Statesman*, January 2002. Shortly afterwards he resigned as chairmen of the Institute of Contemporary Arts.

'ART' is just a racket! A HOAX perpetrated on the public by so-called 'Artists' who set themselves up on a pedestal and promoted by pantywaist ivory-tower intellectuals and sob-sister 'critics' who think the world owes them a living! **Robert Crumb**, *Plunge into the Depths of Despair* (1970)

We've reached the point where Laurence Llewellyn-Bowen might as well be an artist; all he needs is an empty room and some chalk. We pee on things, we pee into things, we pee over things … and call it art. **Brian Sewell**, interviewed in the *Observer*, 13 November 2005

On the Turner Prize:
If this is the best
British artists can
produce then
British art is lost.
Cold, mechanical,
conceptual
bullshit. **Kim Howells**
MP, in 2002, when he was
a junior minister in the
Department of Culture, Media
and Sport

Ranting Movie Reviews

On *Myra Breckinridge* (1970):

Myra Breckinridge is about as funny as a child molester. It is an insult to intelligence, an affront to sensibility and an abomination to the eye. *Time* magazine

On *Apocalypse Now* (1979):

Emotionally obtuse and intellectually empty. Not so much an epic account of a gruelling war as an incongruous, extravagant monument to artistic self-defeat. **Frank Rice**, in *Time*, 1979

> *The worst film ever made ... a film about idiots, made by idiots, for idiots*

On *Stop! Or my Mom will Shoot* (1992):

Maybe one of the worst films in the entire solar system, including alien productions we've never seen ... a flatworm could write a better script ... in some countries – China, I believe – running [the movie] once a week on government television has lowered the birth rate to zero. If they ran it twice a week, I believe in twenty years China would be extinct. **Sylvester Stallone**, who starred in the film

On *An Alan Smithee Film – Burn Hollywood Burn* (1998):

A spectacularly bad film – incompetent, unfunny, ill-conceived, badly executed, lamely written, and acted by people who look trapped in the headlights. **Roger Ebert**

On *Striptease* (1998):

Not funny enough, or dramatic enough, or sexy enough, or bad enough, to qualify as entertainment in any category. **Leonard Maltin**

On *The Master of Disguise* (2002):

This is, without a word of exaggeration, the worst film ever made … a film about idiots, made by idiots, for idiots. **Alan Morrison**, Empireonline.com

Ranting Movie Reviews (continued)

On *Baby Geniuses 2* (2004):

To call this immeasurably terrible movie 'stupid and nonsensical' would be an insult to stupid and nonsensical movies. So thoroughly wrongheaded that it demands a new redefinition of the word 'bad', it features perhaps the worst script I've ever come across, which appears to have been written by an extraterrestrial who not only does not understand English-language idioms or American pop culture but who has a completely alien understanding of concepts such as cause and effect, and hails from an alternate universe in which temporal and spatial relationships are unlike anything we on earth are familiar with. The plot is practically incidental to the awfulness, though on its own is an abomination. **Mary Ann Johanson** on flickfilosopher.com

On *Catwoman* (2004):

A vacuous lingerie show posing as feminism . . . the biggest movie hairball this side of *Garfield*. **Metromix.com**

The biggest movie hairball this side of Garfield

First of all, I want to thank Warner Brothers. Thank you for putting me in a piece of shit, god-awful movie . . . It was just what my career needed. **Halle Berry**, arriving at the Golden Raspberry Awards to receive her Worst Actress 'Razzie' for her performance in *Catwoman*

On *Basic Instinct 2* (2006):

There are inflatable toys that are livelier than [Sharon] Stone, but how can you tell the difference? *Basic Instinct 2* is not an erotic thriller. It is taxidermy. **New York Post**, 2006

Remark reportedly uttered by a critic during a press screening of *The Hottie and the Nottie* (2008), starring Paris Hilton:
Shoot me in the fucking face.

Shoot me in the fucking face

On *Antichrist* (2009):
Antichrist is a horrible combination of extraordinarily unpleasant elements. It's offensively misogynistic. It's needlessly graphic in its use of violence. And its maker almost certainly needs psychiatric help. **Chris Tookey**, *Mail Online*, 24 July 2009

A big, fat art-film fart. *Variety*, May 2009. Reuters reported that at its showing in Cannes, *Antichrist* 'elicited derisive laughter, gasps of disbelief, a smattering of applause and loud boos'.

On *GI Joe* (2009):
… what can I say about *GI Joe*, [Sienna Miller's] new summer blockbuster. Not much, except that it is insultingly inane, cynically commercial and almost unwatchably awful. If you programmed a computer to cobble together a movie out of every cinematic cliché – futuristic weaponry, interminable explosions, leather catsuits – *GI Joe* is pretty much what you would end up with. **Decca Aitkenhead**, in the *Guardian*, 3 August 2009.

It is insultingly inane, cynically commercial and almost unwatchably awful

Marilyn Monroe US actress

She was good at playing abstract confusion in the same way that a midget is good at being short … As far as talent goes, Marilyn Monroe was so minimally gifted as to be unemployable, and anyone who holds to the opinion that she was a great natural comic identifies himself immediately as a dunce. **Clive James**

She is just an arrogant little tail-twitcher

A vacuum with nipples. **Otto Preminger**

I don't think she could act her way out of a paper script. She has no charm, delicacy or taste. She is just an arrogant little tail-twitcher who learned to throw sex in your face. **Nunnally Johnson**, US screenwriter

Michael Moore US documentary maker

Europeans … think Americans are fat, vulgar, greedy, stupid, ambitious and ignorant and so on. And they've taken as their own, as their representative American, someone who actually embodies all of those qualities. **Christopher Hitchens**, on *Scarborough Country*, MSNBC, 19 May 2004

José Mourinho Former Portuguese manager of Chelsea FC

It is vital that the government acts now and destroys him in a controlled explosion. **Harry Pearson**, in the *Guardian*, 7 March 2005

Robert Mugabe Zimbabwean tyrant

The capricious, mendacious, pocket-stuffing old lunatic. **Euan Ferguson**, in the *Observer*, 20 March 2005

Rupert Murdoch Australian-born international media tycoon

No self-respecting fish would want to be wrapped in a Murdoch newspaper. **George Royko**

That drivel-merchant, global huckster and so-to-speak media psychopath Rupert Murdoch, a Hannibal the Cannibal who is in many important ways a deal more powerful in Britain than our own schoolboy Parliament, its minority-elected government and even its bumbling Mr Pooter of a prime minister … If we cared tuppence about our own culture, we ought to make sure that the next time Murdoch sets foot in this, his fiefdom, he should be arrested and put on public trial. **Dennis Potter**, on Channel 4, 1993. 'Mr Pooter' is a reference to the then prime minister, John Major.

Andy Murray Scottish tennis player

Can Andy Murray and Jamie Murray really be related? Sure, the two Scotsmen have physical similarities, but look again – Jamie's smile, Andy's scowl; Jamie's rounded, pleasing face; Andy's dolichocephalic … Donald Duck features. Andy … plays with his face frozen into a grimace. He blames everybody for his failings (mother, coach, the Davis Cup) but himself …

Everything about him reeks of petulance

While the game has had its share of bad-tempered or po-faced champs, they have usually had something about them – Ilie Nastase and John McEnroe were rude but they had chutzpah and wit; Martina Navratilova and Bjorn Borg didn't smile much but they had soul. All Andy has at the moment is his petulance. Everything about him reeks of petulance – even his sideburns and bum-fluff tache … wouldn't it be strange if, after all the years of Henmania and near misses, he turned out to be the first British player to win Wimbledon since Fred Perry in the mid-16th century and nobody gave a toss? **Simon Hattenstone**, in the *Guardian*, 20 February 2008

From
Nanny
to
Norway

Nanny Knows Best Driving with a cold is as bad as driving under the influence of drink and drugs, so the 'experts' tell us. Just wait until the Mad Mullah hears about this. Every 'flu season, the Traffic Taliban will be setting up roadblocks and stopping anyone suspected of mainlining Lemsip. **Richard Littlejohn**, on *Mail Online*, 3 February 2009

Just wait until the Mad Mullah hears about this

In the entry for 7 July 2011 in 'The diary of Old Holborn aged 46 and three-quarters':
12:00 Pop to the shop. Tesco have fitted RF scanners and like an idiot I took my wife's ID card by mistake so apart from greeting me like a woman, the shopping trolley informs me that I need tampons. Wonderful. If I don't buy them, a message will be sent to her GP informing them that she needs a hysterectomy or some such shite. Bollocks. If I have her ID card, I won't be able to buy my daily ration of beer either. She only gets 12 units a week and the scanner will reject it. Arse. Apparently we have used too much mustard as well … **grumpieroldmen.co.uk**, 8 July 2008

Some people, though, are prepared to challenge the anti-nanny-state ranters:
I've never quite understood how the *Daily Mail* tallies its 'rip-off Britain/nanny state/PC-gone-mad' rants with its 'something must be done about immigrants/house prices/cancer/ban-this-filth-now' rants. Aren't they completely contradictory? Who's going to 'do something' about this stuff if not the 'nanny state'?
'della_duckboarder', on London *Evening Standard* messageboard, 21 July 2009

New Age
Sedona, Arizona. Home of beautiful red rock canyons, scenic desert landscapes ... and every crystal-sucking, vortex-fucking asshole out to make a few bucks off of New Age hippie bullshit! **Penn Fraser Jillette**, on the TV show *Penn & Teller: Bullshit!*

The key word for me – my spleen isn't really big enough to explode with all the splenetic juices of fury that drive me when I consider this – but the real key word that triggers my rage is the word 'energy', when people start talking about it in terms of negative or positive types. For instance, 'There's very negative energy in here.' What are you talking about? What do you mean? I mean, let's think about it. What does energy mean? Well, we know what it means: energy from petrol when it's burned, it moves the car. 'This room has positive energy' — well, where the fuck's it going then? It's not moving. It's covering up such woolly thinking, such pathetic nonsense ... **Stephen Fry**, on *Room 101*

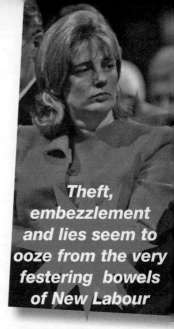

Theft, embezzlement and lies seem to ooze from the very festering bowels of New Labour

New Labour
These people are moral and political pygmies ... New Labour are scum. **Craig Murray**, British ambassador in Tashkent until removed by the Foreign Office after he had attacked the human-rights record of the government of Uzbekistan, an ally in Britain and America's 'war on terror'

On New Labour's antenatal period:
Turn for some crumb of comfort
to the Labour Party? Forget it! The
Labour Party seem to be packaging
themselves like a pack of toilet paper at
the moment, sort of going for this pastel
politics look. This sort of – Labour, little
rose, a kind of tampon that uses the same
logo called 'Femmes'. Perhaps it would be even
less socialist to call themselves Labs – Labbies – 'Safe, strong, soft
Neil Kinnock absorbs all kinds of shit except socialism.' Expands
width-wise to include everybody.   **Linda Smith**, *Linda Live*, 1986

Absorbs all kinds of shit except socialism

As Blair and his impertinent young political pups wage war on old Labour … as they seek to kill off their fathers, these political adolescents boost themselves with a dangerous amnesiac and, thus drugged, the courageous volunteers, damned with piss-proud erections, dare to obliterate the reality that the most 'radical and regenerative Labour government' that brought us the welfare state, was led by old men. **Leo Abse**, a Labour MP from 1958 to 1987

Nouvelle cuisine was French for 'Fucking hell, is that all you get?' This is Nouvelle Labour. **Rory Bremner**

They are indeed a foul disgusting party. Theft, embezzlement and lies seem to ooze from the very festering bowels of New Labour. They are a party who sailed in on a sea of lies and deception, and they will sail out, full and bloated, on the same foul sea that fetched them up. **'Rommel'**, on Yahoo! Answers

New York People'll say the stupidest things sometimes too, 'Hey, man, if you quit smoking you get your sense of smell back.'

I live in New York City, I got news for you – I don't want my fucking sense of smell back. [*Sniffs*] Is that urine? [*Sniffs*] I think I smell a dead guy! Honey, look, a dead guy! Covered in urine, check this out! Someone just pee'd on this guy, that's fresh. Just think, if I'd been smoking I never would have found him! A urine-covered dead fella, what're the odds? Thank God I quit smoking, now I can enjoy the wonders of New York, honey, look! US satirist **Bill Hicks**

A urine-covered dead fella, what're the odds?

New York has more commissioners than Des Moines, Iowa, has residents, including the Commissioner for Making Sure the Sidewalks Are Always Blocked by Steaming Fetid Mounds of Garbage the Size of the Appalachian Foothills, and, of course, the Commissioner for Bicycle Messengers Bearing Down on You at Warp Speed with Mohawk Haircuts and Pupils Smaller Than Purely Theoretical Particles … **Dave Barry**

New Zealand A poxy little island in the Pacific Ocean.
Scott Johnson, Australian assistant coach to the Welsh rugby team, in 2004

The 1960s
On the legacy of the 60s:
We allowed our patriotism to be turned into a joke, wise sexual restraint to be mocked as prudery, our families to be defamed as nests of violence, loathing and abuse, our literature to be tossed aside as so much garbage, and our church turned into a department of the social security system … **Peter Hitchens**, *The Abolition of Britain* (1999)

The 1980s

In the eighties it was not fashionable to stand up for anything. It was a decade where bending over was the thing you did to get ahead. The way up the ladder was with your mouth attached to the anal orifice of the creature – whatever its denomination – in front of you.

The way up the ladder was with your mouth attached to the anal orifice of the creature in front of you

It was pushing upward and sucking at the same time as you went up the rungs, with junk bonds spilling out of your pockets and your mind reeling from the LSD experience that you had had in the sixties … It was an era where there was enough cash and enough movement up and down in the stock market and enough shady deals that these incompetent little shit-heads were able to make vast amounts of money to buy their Ferraris and snort their cocaine and ruin the economy … People wish that the good old days of the eighties would come back. When there was still something to steal.   **Frank Zappa**, 1992

Richard Nixon

Disgraced 37th President of the USA   Richard Nixon is a no-good lying bastard. He can lie out of both sides of his mouth at the same time and if he ever caught himself telling the truth he'd lie just to keep his hand in.   **Harry S. Truman**, 33rd President of the USA

For years I've regarded his existence as a monument to all the rancid genes and broken chromosomes that corrupt the possibilities of the American Dream; he was a foul caricature of himself, a man with no soul, no inner convictions, with the integrity of a hyena and the style of a poison toad. The Nixon I remembered was absolutely humorless; I couldn't imagine him laughing at anything except maybe a paraplegic who wanted to vote Democratic but couldn't quite reach the lever on the voting machine. **Hunter S. Thompson**, in *Pageant*, July 1968

The integrity of a hyena and the style of a poison toad

Richard Nixon is a pubic hair in the teeth of America. **Graffito**

Avoid all needle drugs – the only dope worth shooting is Richard Nixon. **Abbie Hoffman**, *Steal this Book* (1971)

Nixon was so crooked that he needed servants to help him screw his pants on every morning

If the right people had been in charge of Nixon's funeral, his casket would have been launched into one of those open-sewage canals that empty into the ocean just south of Los Angeles. He was a swine of a man and a jabbering dupe of a president. Nixon was so crooked that he needed servants to help him screw his pants on every morning. Even his funeral was illegal. He was queer in the deepest way. His body should have been burned in a trash bin. **Hunter S. Thompson**, in *Rolling Stone*, June 1994

The North and Northerners

Northerners are far too busy breeding pigeons, eating deep-fried chip butties and executing drive-by shootings on Moss Side to dally over the new Sebastian Faulks. **Hildy Johnson**, in the *Bookseller*, 9 March 2001

People in the North die of ignorance and crisps. **Edwina Currie**, when she was junior health minister, September 1986

The North of England is underrated in my view. You can leave your door open, because there's nothing worth nicking anyway. A tin bath and a box set of Adam Sandler videos.
Frankie Boyle

People in the North die of ignorance and chips

Northern Ireland

For God's sake, someone bring me a large Scotch. What a bloody awful country. **Reginald Maudling**, Conservative Home Secretary, returning from the province to London, 1 July 1970

What a bloody awful country

Norway

Fuck off, Norway. **Paul Gascoigne**, asked on live TV before an England–Norway World Cup qualifier if he had a message for the Norwegian people

I don't like Norwegians at all. The sun never sets, the bar never opens, and the whole country smells of kippers. **Evelyn Waugh**, letter to Lady Diana Cooper, 13 July 1934

That Norwegian Football Commentator's Rant

Yurrrgggggh!!! Der stod Ingelland!!! Lord Nelson!!! Lord Beaverbrook!!! Winston Churchill!!! Henry Cooper!!! Clement Attlee!!! Anthony Eden!!! Lady Diana!!! Der stod dem all!!! Der stod dem all!!! Maggie Thatcher, can you hear me? Can you hear me, Maggie? Your boys took one hell of a beating tonight!!! **Norwegian commentator Borg Lillelien** celebrates Norway's 2–1 victory over England in 1981

Your boys took one hell of a beating tonight!!!

*O@!

From
Obama
to
Owen

Barack Obama 44th President of the USA I want to cut his nuts off. **Rev. Jesse Jackson,** on Fox News, July 2008, not realizing he was being recorded. He later said that his support for Obama was 'wide, deep and unequivocal'.

Old People Something must be said; something must be done! Old people are wearing too much beige. There I've said it now. I may make some enemies with these words but I simply can't bear it anymore; the sight of a Saga coach shedding its passengers and they're all wearing beige; beige anoraks, beige overcoats, beige hats, beige trousers; it's obscene. (The very word 'beige' is obscene; being impossible to pronounce except with a mild French accent. I even believe it means 'the colour of the liquid that oozes out of the small intestine'.) **Rory McGrath,** grumpieroldmen. co.uk., 27 April 2005

Old people are wearing too much beige

Those stringback, driving-glove-clad dullards who yearn for the return of National Service … these tiresome old farts. **Matthew Norman,** in the *Evening Standard,* 26 April 2004

All of a sudden there are geezers and duffers and biddies everywhere you look. There didn't used to be this many old people. page 210

Elderly fools

Ozzie Osbourne

English heavy metal musician

Embracing his wife Sharon:
Merry Xmas. Now fuck off.

When one of his dogs relieves itself in his bedroom:
Who pissed!? Who pissed on my fucking carpet!!? That bastard fucking dog, man. I'm going to throw you in the pool! Get the fuck out of my house! Why do they do it, Sharon? What's the deal, man? It's a fucking terrorist man! It's fucking part of Bin Laden's gang! Fucking Ali Baba used to go work on this rug.

When Sharon suggested foam as part of his stage act:
Bubbles!? Oh come on, Sharon! I'm fucking Ozzie Osbourne, I'm the Prince of fucking Darkness. Evil! Evil! What's fucking evil about a shitload of bubbles!? On *The Osbournes* TV show

On the famous incident when he bit off a bat's head on stage:
It took a lot of water to down just that fucking bat's head, let me tell you. It's still stuck in my fucking throat, after all these years. People all over the world say, 'You're the guy who kills creatures? You still do it? You do it every night?' It happened fucking once, for Christ's sake. Interviewed in *Rolling Stone* online, May 1997

> *I'm the Prince of fucking Darkness. Evil! Evil!*

I remember when it was just the occasional coot on a porch rocker waxing nostalgic about outdoor plumbing. Now they're all over the place – arteriosclerosing around on the racquet-ball courts, badgering skydiving instructors for senior-citizen discounts, hogging the Jacuzzi at the singles apartment complex. They're even taking over pop music. I went to see The Who last summer, and a bunch of old farts were playing in the band. **P.J. O'Rourke**, 1992

> *I went to see The Who last summer, and a bunch of old farts were playing in the band*

Just heard in the news that in ten years' time they'll be more pensioners than young people. What a terrifying statistic for the country's paedophiles. No wonder Gary Glitter didn't want to come back. What we should do to deal with this problem is to actually pay pensioners extra to take up really dangerous sports, like rollerblading through safari parks wearing suits made of ham. **Frankie Boyle**

Yoko Ono Japanese artist John Lennon gets six bullets in the chest. Yoko Ono, standing right next to him, not one fucking bullet. Will you explain that to me, God? **Denis Leary**

If I found her floating in my pool, I'd punish my dog. **Joan Rivers**, quoted in the *Independent*, 24 January 1996

Opera An interminable session of sweaty, fat Italians shouting about their dead wives. **Dom Joly**, in the *Independent*, 12 September 2004

George Osborne Shadow Chancellor of the Exchequer, born Gideon Oliver Osborne What is really jarring though, is Gideon, who was born into a family of millionaires, who was privately educated at St Paul's, who was in the Bullingdon Club at Oxford (as were Cameron and Boris), where the coat and tails uniform costs £3,000, the main purpose of the group being to get drunk and commit acts of vandalism, and then just pay off the victims of this vandalism the next day, who spent 4 days with Russian billionaire Oleg Deripaska on his luxury yacht, [allegedly] trying to get a donation off him to the Tory party – for this man, who has lead this sort of life, to attack ordinary people for having 'excessive' lifestyles is obscene, and about as hypocritical as you can get. Why is no one throwing green slime over this poisonous, vile, smug Tory git? **'Phil'**, 8 March 2009, on Everybody Hates Tories open group on Facebook

Michael Owen English footballer This man – what's his name? – the number 10, the small one who doesn't play in the Real Madrid first team – said that if Poland beat Azerbaijan 8–0, England should score at least eight and he'd score five of them … Who is Michael Owen anyway? What has he ever won in football? He plays for Real Madrid but he is always on the bench. I have a history in football, but what is the history of this guy, this midget? He ought to clean his tongue and wash the boots of David Beckham as they are so wet tonight. He didn't score one. Sven-Göran Eriksson is a good man, he should teach him to respect everyone. Who is he anyway? Who is he? … He's a midget and I am not prepared to discuss him any longer. Azerbaijan manager and former Brazilian star **Carlos Alberto**, March 2005. He wrongly thought Owen had claimed he would score five goals against his side in a World Cup qualifier.

From
Palin
to
Provincials

Sarah Palin Republican vice-presidential candidate Sarah Palin has me and my friends retching in our handbags. She's such a power-mad backwater beauty-pageant casualty, it's easy to write her off and make fun of her, but in reality, I feel as horrified as a ghetto Jew watching the rise of National Socialism. **Cintra Wilson**, in *Salon* online magazine, 2008

She's going to have the nuclear codes

I think there's a really good chance that Sarah Palin could be president. I think that's the really scary thing … I know that she was mayor of a really, really small town. And she was governor of Alaska for less than two years … I think the pick was made for political purposes. But in terms of governance, it's a disaster. You do the actuary tables, there's a one out of three chance, if not more, that McCain doesn't survive his first term, and it'll be President Palin. I was talking about it earlier. It's like a really bad Disney movie. The hockey mom. Oh, I'm just a hockey mom from Alaska, and she's president. She's facing down Vladimir Putin and using the folksy stuff she learned at the hockey rink. It's absurd. It's totally absurd, and I don't understand why more people aren't talking about how absurd it is. It's a really terrifying possibility. The fact that we've got this far, and we're that close to this being a reality, is crazy. Crazy … I need to know if she really thinks dinosaurs were here 4,000 years ago. That's … important … I want to know that. I really do. Because she's going to have the nuclear codes. I want to know if she thinks dinosaurs were here 4,000 years ago. Or if she banned books or tried to ban books. You know, we can't have that. **Matt Damon** speaks to *The Associated Press*, September 2008

Serial Ranter no. 10

Ian Paisley

Ulster clergyman and politician

No surrender! A frequently enunciated slogan of Ulster Protestant defiance, harking back to the Siege of Londonderry in 1689

We are not prepared to stand idly by and be murdered in our beds!! Another slogan

Heckling Pope John Paul II during a visit to the European Parliament, October 1988:
I denounce you, Antichrist!!!! I refuse you as Christ's enemy and Antichrist with all your false doctrine!!!!!

In 1968 he said of Ulster Catholics:
They breed like rabbits and multiply like vermin!!!!!!!

Resisting moves to legalize homosexuality in N. Ireland:
Save Ulster from sodomy!!!!!!!

On enjoying oneself:
Line dancing is as sinful as any other type of dancing, with its sexual gestures and touching. It is an incitement to lust!!!!!!!!

The gloves are off. We're taking no more nonsense from anybody!!!!

This so-called peace process … is really a surrender process!!!!!!!!!!

Of the leader of Sinn Féin, in 1997:
I will never sit down with Gerry Adams … he'd sit with anyone. He'd sit down with the devil. In fact, Adams does sit down with the devil!!!!!!!!!!!!!

Save Ulster from sodomy!!!!!!!

Gwyneth Paltrow   American actress

On her GOOP 'lifestyle website' (tagline: 'Nourish the inner aspect'):

Lady, you should take your macrobiotic recipes with their expensive ingredients and shove them up your yogariffic ass. Talk about tone deaf! Debuting this website the week after a stock market crash shows that Paltrow is about as publicly savvy as Marie Antoinette.   **'Jessica',** on jezebel.com

Paltrow kicked back in the March 2009 edition of *Elle*:

Fuck the haters! I saw this blog of people writing horrible things about me and for a second your ego is so wounded … How could people hate me, my intentions or what I'm trying to do? I'm a good person and I'm trying to put good things into the world …

Pandering to the Mob

Left to the court of public opinion, we'd bring back hanging, restore the grammar schools, end immigration … We'd pull out of Europe, scrap the yuman rites act and put every foreign criminal and terrorist on the first plane to Timbuktu … Serial burglars, car thieves and anyone carrying an offensive weapon in public would face automatic, exemplary prison sentences. Ludicrous elf'n'safety laws would be scrapped and the legions of five-a-day coordinators and diversity managers would have their contracts torn up and be told to get a proper job …   **Richard Littlejohn,** *Mail Online*, 3 March 2009

Bring back hanging, restore the grammar schools, end immigration

Pekinese Dogs Right in front of me was this little two-inch ball of fluff, a Pekinese, he's the John Selwyn Gummer of the animal kingdom. They're like a Sony Walkman, they're very small but they make a lot of noise. *Yap yap yap yap yap yap yap*. And his name was Yappy.

If this dog should dare to roam, run it over because we bloody hate it

I knew his name was Yappy, because he had a lovely little collar on and it said 'This dog's name is Yappy. If this dog should dare to roam, run it over *because we bloody hate it.*' Little small noisy dogs, nobody likes them, we all hate them. And where do they come from? They seem to sort of *emerge* from rich old ladies' armpits, sort of grow out of their fur coats going 'Yap yap yap give me some more sweets, give me some more cake, pamper me or I'll run away, and then you'll be sad cos I'm your only friend aren't I?' Evil dogs. But it's not their fault, they were bred, they're mutations, two thousand years ago in China some dildo decided to cross a wolf with a gerbil, and the result was the first Pekinese … There's mum, some great big butch Chinese she-wolf, hadn't even noticed when Jeremy Gerbil had done the business. 'Hello, mum!' 'What the *hell* are you?' 'I'm your child!' 'Naff off, you're embarrassing me.' … **Ben Elton**, on *Saturday Live*, 1986

London

London A noisy, dirty place where you are going to be ripped off by greedy shopkeepers and hoteliers, a dump, in other words. **Richard Ingrams**, in the *Observer*, 17 July 2005

Jolly old London … consists almost entirely of looming grey building-shaped objects constructed from bin lids and misery. **Charlie Brooker**, in the *Guardian*, 25 May 2009

This God-forsaken hell-hole

Manchester He chose to live in Manchester, a totally incomprehensible choice for any free human being to make. **Sir Melford Stevenson**, English judge, quoted in the *Daily Telegraph*, 11 April 1979

Middlesex Imagine coming from Middlesex. What a terrible, terrible thing to have to live with. **Yorkshire-born Jeremy Paxman**

Nottingham A putrid tumour of social rot in the heart of England. **'jdennis_99'**, chavtowns.co.uk, January 2006

It has the ugliest provincial city centre I have ever seen, designed without care, or feeling, or even eyesight, such is its encrustation of visual pollution. **Gideon Haigh** on cricinfo.com, 25 August 2005

Peterborough

It's horrible, and not in a funny way, just a bad way. I wrote the entire book without going there and then went for a night to check a few details. I stayed at a hotel. There's nothing I can say apart from: don't do that. I tried to go to a restaurant; there are no restaurants in Peterborough. **Mark Haddon**, whose novel, *A Spot of Bother* is set in Peterborough; quoted in the *Observer*, 27 August 2006

Southend-on-Sea

Southend isn't really on the sea but the Thames estuary. Like you couldn't tell from the garbage- and muck-strewn 'beach'. Parents can often be seen trying to pretend they have taken their kids to a real seaside resort by putting them in swimming costumes … But no one dares enter the stagnant puddle-water that is the sea. **Diana McCar**

Weston-super-Mare

This God-forsaken hell-hole of a resort … The way I see it, there are three reasons never to be unhappy. First you were born … Second, you are alive … Third, you have plenty to eat, you live in a time of peace and 'Tie a Yellow Ribbon Round the Old Oak Tree' will never be number one again. If you bear these things in mind, you will never be truly unhappy – though in fairness I must point out that if you find yourself alone in Weston-super-Mare on a rainy Tuesday evening you may come close. **Bill Bryson**, *Notes from a Small Island* (1995)

Yorkshire

A huddle of cows are gloating in front of me. A gaggle of chickens is shrieking with laughter behind me. I am in hell. I am in a place called Yorkshire. **Johann Hari**, 1 October 2004

Prince Philip The Duke of Edinburgh runs the country behind the scenes; he is the actual head of the Royal Family. He's a racist, he grew up with Nazis, and one of his aunts married one of Hitler's generals. Beneath the surface he has a German name – Frankenstein. Well it sounds like Frankenstein. **Mohammed al Fayed**, at the Princess Diana inquest, February 2008. He also described the Windsors as 'that Dracula family', and Camilla Parker Bowles as a 'crocodile wife'.

Kevin Pietersen South-African born England batsman It would be a surprise if the mirrors in Pietersen's house totalled anything less the entire stock at one of the larger branches of B & Q, and though it is not uncommon nowadays for the voice from the bedroom calling out: 'I'll be down in a minute darling, I'm just putting in my ear-rings' to be a male one, not many would fork out £25,000 for a pair of diamond encrusted ones shaped like cricket balls. Pietersen's bodily adornments also extend to tattoos, though fashion has moved away from the sailor about to go to sea with 'I Love Gladys' or 'MUFC' inked into his forearm. He has gone for three lions and

Little Shit Parris vs Big Cunt Campbell

I'd rather be a little shit than a big cunt

In his published diaries, Alastair Campbell, formerly Tony Blair's press secretary, mentioned a meeting with Matthew Parris, the parliamentary sketch writer and former Tory MP:

The little shit Parris ... with that perma-smirk on his face.

Parris responded:

I'd rather be a little shit than a big cunt.

a number representing his status as the 626th player to be capped by England … His hairdresser gets a bit confused as well, one day required to turn his client's coiffeur into a furry animal and the next a field of farmer's stubble … **Martin Johnson**, in the *Daily Telegraph*, 13 May 2006

On Pietersen's autobiography *Crossing the Boundary*, for which Ebury Press paid a reported advance of £300,000:
This book is a study in narcissism and should be avoided at all costs by people who care about the game of cricket … It is hard to overstate the banality of the ghosted prose. **Peter Oborne**, in 'Cricket Books, 2006', *Wisden* 2007

Political Correctness

Political correctness has changed everything. People forget that political correctness used to be called spastic gay talk. **Frankie Boyle**, on *Mock the Week*

It's everybody's political right to speak abominably

Political Correctness: A doctrine … which holds forth the proposition that it is entirely possible to pick up a turd by the clean end. **Anon**.

The talk I hear among civilized people, which used to be fairly grammatical until about twelve or fifteen years ago, has now gone completely to pot … Now if terrible grammar is used, it's justified by liberal or leftist politics: it's everybody's political right to speak abominably as he or she wishes. There's an organized pull towards undermining language whether it's by feminists, homosexuals, or some ethnic minority whose attempts to undermine English are considered their God-given or state-given right. **John Simon**, US critic, 1987

Politics and Politicians What disgusts me …

is the lackadaisical attitude shown by some Hon Members toward the truth and the clichés spouted by some of the unbelievably useless creatures we elect to the Commons. **Quentin Letts**, *Mail Online*, 9 January 2006

A horrible voice, bad breath and a vulgar manner – the characteristics of a popular politician. **Aristophanes**, Ancient Greek playwright

A palm-pounding pack of preening pols. **William Safire** on US congressmen

The unbelievably useless creatures we elect to the Commons

The word 'politics' is derived from the word 'poly', meaning 'many', and the word 'ticks', meaning 'blood-sucking parasites'. **Larry Hardiman**

Ricky Ponting Captain of the Australian cricket team Ponting is

a smartarse and a disgrace as leader. The conduct of him and his players is absolutely disgraceful. He has no control over his players. The standard of conduct that was commonplace in my time has been contemptuously trampled underfoot …
Lou Rowan, Australian test umpire from 1963 to 1971, in the Sydney *Herald Sun*, January 2006

After Gary Pratt, a substitute fielder, ran him out in a 2005 Ashes Test, Ponting ranted:
I think it is an absolute disgrace the spirit of the game is being treated like that … Being here in England they've obviously got the resources to just draft in the best fieldsmen that they possibly

can at the time. The way they've been doing it is just before
their bowlers are about to bowl they'll send them off for a short
amount of time to have a bit of a loosen-up and a massage and
that sort of stuff, and come back on and bowl … It's within the
rules of the game but it's just not within the spirit of the game,
which is what we're all trying to uphold. **Ricky Ponting**, August 2005.
Duncan Fletcher, England's coach, responded: 'You want to take a run to a cover fielder and
get run out, whose fault is that? You know what's more? All the palaver caused me to burn
my toast.'

Pro-lifers
You know who's really bugging me these days.
These pro-lifers … You ever look at their faces? 'I'm pro-life!'
'I'm pro-life!' Boy, they look it don't they? They just exude *joie de
vivre*. You just want to hang with them and play Trivial Pursuit
all night long. You know what bugs me about them? If you're
so pro-life, do me a favour – don't lock arms and block medical
clinics. If you're so pro-life, lock arms and block cemeteries. Let's
see how committed you are to this idea.

> *Pro-lifer*: She can't come in!
> *Confused member of funeral procession*: She was 98. She was hit
> by a bus!
> *Pro-lifer*: There's options!
> *Confused member of funeral procession*: What else can we do?
> Have her stuffed?

I want to see pro-lifers with crowbars at funerals opening caskets
– 'Get out!' Then I'd be really impressed by their mission. **Bill Hicks**

Provincials
I'm going to ruin your day and garrotte you.
Because I'm a Londoner and you're all wankers. **Marcus Brigstocke**

John Prescott New Labour politician

He couldn't wear a tie and a belt in the same day or he'd turn into sausages.

Frankie Boyle, on *Mock the Week*

Treats the English language like a novice customer in a spaghetti house.

Quentin Letts, *Mail Online*, 9 January 2006

I suspect language isn't his first language.

Linda Smith

He couldn't wear a tie and a belt in the same day or he'd turn into sausages

From
Racing
to
RyanAir

Racing Commentators
A bunch of insular, snobby, sonorous farts twittering on about how lovely the Queen Mother looked at Ascot. **Matthew Norman**, in the *Evening Standard*, 17 January 2005, on the species prior to the advent of John McCririck

Paula Radcliffe
British marathon runner I liked the way that the Great Britain Olympic team got off the plane in the order of how many medals they won. Paula Radcliffe must have been stuck in one of the overhead lockers. Saying that, it's not all that bad for Paula. If she was a horse, she would have been shot by now. **Frankie Boyle**

If she was a horse, she would have been shot by now

Sir Walter Raleigh
English courtier and adventurer I will prove you the notoriousest traitor that ever came to the Bar … thou art a monster … the most vile and execrable traitor that ever lived. I want words sufficient to express thy viperous treasons. Thou art an odious fellow, thy name is hateful to all the realm of England … There never lived a viler viper upon the face of the earth than thou.
Sir Edward Coke, prosecuting Raleigh for treason, 1601

Serial Ranter no. 11
Gordon Ramsay
Scottish celebrity chef

Sundry remarks addressed to participants on the US version of *Hell's Kitchen*:
That is absolute dog shit … You're a plank … You have a palate like a cow's backside. That is disgusting … That looks like a dog's dinner … This is fucking painful! … If you haven't tasted your own fucking food, what chance have you got? I'd rather fuck off for a burger!

To a maître d':
Every time I see you it's like this! Like a baby rhinoceros trying to take a shit!

I'd rather fuck off for a burger!

On the Yorkshire pudding offered up by a participant on *Ramsay's Kitchen Nightmares*:
It looks like King Kong's fucking condom!

On reading a press release from a hotel in Scotland announcing that they are serving up a deep-fried Nutella sandwich:
I'm horrified. I mean, Christ! Seventy-five per cent of my staff are French. They look at me like I'm some sort of twat that my Scottish brothers are launching two slices of bread with a fucking inch of Nutella between them, battered and deep-fat fried. Now what the fuck is this country coming to? What are we doing to ourselves? That has to be abolished. Here we are, progressing tenfold, buying the right bread, real croissants, we're making fresh muesli and we understand what a great cup of coffee is. And then some idiot

brings out a deep-fried chocolate sandwich. I want to find the bastard that put that idea together. I've got the most amazing charcoal grill in my new kitchen. I'm going to sit his butt on it and criss-cross my name on his bloody arse cheeks to remind him. Every time he wakes up in the morning he can gawp at his arse. Is he fucking stupid? When these things hit France, the French just have a field day laughing at us. So I'm looking for that scumbag. I'm going to fucking grill his arse. Brand him with a hot iron like a little calf or a lamb. I'm going to put Ramsayfied on his butt, so every time he wakes up in the morning, he thinks 'Fuck! I shouldn't have done that!'

> **I'm looking for that scumbag. I'm going to fucking grill his arse**

On dining at the Palace:

You don't actually know who's cooking for the Queen, but I'd never employ him because the food was shit. The food was shit but she was lovely. Unfortunately you've got to go through the ceremony with the canapés which are absolutely, shockingly shit.

Gordon Ramsay (continued)

They looked prehistoric, like 300 years old, at Buckingham Palace … I was trying to get rid of it [some duck liver pâté] as I was approaching her because this thing was taking forever to chew. You couldn't spit it out on the carpet, for God's sake …

Quoted in thelondonpaper.com

On rival celebrity chef Antony Worrall Thompson:
A squashed Bee Gee … can't cook to save his life. Quoted in Mirror.co.uk

Some of Ramsay's rivals are capable of out-ranting him. Raymond Blanc, for example, was not amused when Ramsay's TV production sent him a letter asking if he would like to appear on a forthcoming series of *Ramsay's Kitchen Nightmares*.
Ramsay recounts what happened next:

He was on a mailing list and he went fucking mad. I had a message from this Frenchman on my mobile phone in LA in August and it was *'Putain! Qu'est-ce que tu fais? Wanker!'* I mean, he didn't see it as a funny joke so I apologised. Interview with Elizabeth Day for the *Observer Food Monthly*

Putain! Qu'est-ce que tu fais? Wanker!

In June 2009 Ramsay caused a furore when he attacked Australian TV personality Tracy Grimshaw, dubbed 'Australia's answer to Fern Britton'. While being interviewed on her show, he commented on a mole on her face:
Is that a wart? It looks like your little sister is on your lip.

At a food and wine show the following day in Melbourne, he pointed to a picture of a woman on her hands and knees with multiple breasts and the face of a pig and said: That's Tracy Grimshaw … I had an interview with her yesterday. Holy crap, she needs to see Simon Cowell's Botox doctor.

Grimshaw's subsequent response to these remarks included the following: How many people would laugh if they were effectively described as an old, ugly pig? I spent all day yesterday trying to think about how to respond and I thought about saying nothing. But we all know that bullies thrive when no one takes them on. I am not going to sit meekly and let some arrogant narcissist bully me … We have all seen how Gordon Ramsay treats his wife and he supposedly loves her. We are all just fodder to him … Obviously Gordon thinks that any woman who doesn't find him attractive must be gay. For the record, I don't. And I'm not.

Outraged Australian PM Kevin Rudd said of Ramsay: I think I can describe his remarks as reflecting a new form of low life.

A new form of low life

Even Ramsay's mother Helen was horrified, to the extent that she phoned up Ramsay and told him in no uncertain terms to apologise. Which he did, unreservedly, telling the Australian media: She was disgusted … When your mum rings you and starts to give you a bollocking down the telephone than of course you start to get the picture …

Ronald Reagan   40th President of the USA   The biggest threat
to America today is not communism. It's moving America toward
a fascist theocracy, and everything that's happened during the
Reagan administration is steering us right down that pipe …
When you have a government that prefers a certain moral code
derived from a certain religion and that moral code turns into
legislation to suit one certain religious point of view, and if that
code happens to be very, very right wing, almost toward Attila the
Hun …   **Frank Zappa**, in 1986

Reality TV   There is just
no escaping this torture. It is
EVERYWHERE. Ever seen the
film *28 Days Later* … ? There's
a virus called RAGE that sends
people mental and extremely
violent. I know where this comes
from. The other day *Big Brother*
started its latest series. I decided to
watch a little bit for some rant fodder,
and to see what massive wankers are involved
this time. It wasn't pretty. I can remember twitching after five
minutes, then blanking out. I awoke ten minutes later and found
that I'd put my foot through the TV and completely trashed
the room.   **itsallbollox.com**, on yet another series of *Big Brother*

*I awoke
ten minutes
later and found
that I'd put my
foot through
the TV*

Real Madrid   The most educated person
at Real Madrid is the woman who
cleans the lavatories.   **Joan Gaspart**,
vice-president of Barcelona, in 1997

Referees   I never comment on referees and I'm not going to break the habit of a lifetime for that prat. **Ron Atkinson** in 1979

On the referee John Toro Rendon:

An infantile Colombian coffee-picker wearing a dunce's hat and holding a FIFA referee's certificate. FIFA should immediately return him home to the coffee plantations and drug kings for a life sentence with the message never to show up at a World Cup again. The Danish tabloid newspaper *BT*, after Rendon had sent off two Danish players in Denmark's game against Saudi Arabia in the 1998 World Cup

> *An infantile Colombian coffee-picker wearing a dunce's hat*

On the Swiss referee Urs Meier:

A preening pompadour with the looks of a gay porn star.
David Mellor, in the *Evening Standard*, 25 June 2004, after Meier had disallowed a goal by Sol Campbell in the Euro 2004 England–Portugal quarter final

Shame on the Swiss referee, the Emmenthal-eating appeasement monkey who ruined the lives of millions of honest yeomen bearing their simple flag. **Justin Cartwright**, in the *Evening Standard*, 25 June 2004

Religion   God is a cloacal accumulation of stupidity.
Euan Ferguson, in the *Observer*, 24 September 2006

This one goes out to the followers of the three Abrahamic
religions, to the Muslims, Christians and Jews. Just a little thing
really, but d'you think that when you've finished smashing up
the world and blowing each other to bits and demanding special
privileges while you do it, d'you think maybe that the rest of us
could sort of have our planet back? I wouldn't ask, but the thing
is I'm starting to think there must be something written in the
special books each of you so enjoy referring
to that tells you it's alright to behave
like precious, petulant, pugnacious
pricks. Forgive the alliteration but
your persistent power-mad punch-
ups are pissing me off.   **Marcus
Brigstocke**, on BBC Radio 4's *The Now Show*

*You could
be in the
Garden of Eden
if you had just
kept your fucking
mouth shut*

Judaism … along with Islam and
Christianity … does insist that
some turgid and contradictory and
sometimes evil and mad texts, obviously
written by fairly unexceptional humans, are in fact the word of
God.   **Christopher Hitchens**, *Letters to a Young Contrarian* (2001)

Religion … comes from the bawling and fearful infancy of our
species, and is a babyish attempt to meet our inescapable demand
for knowledge. Today the least educated of my children knows
much more about the natural order than any of the founders of
religion.   **Christopher Hitchens**, *God Is Not Great: How Religion Poisons Everything* (2007)

The essence of Christianity is told to us in the Garden of
Eden history. The fruit that was forbidden was on the Tree of
Knowledge. The subtext is, All the suffering you have is because
you wanted to find out what was going on. You could be in the
Garden of Eden if you had just kept your fucking mouth shut and
hadn't asked any questions. **Frank Zappa**, interviewed in *Playboy*, 2 May 1993

Islam would be a far more attractive religion if it simply asked
three things of its adherents, namely: (a) make up lovely Kinder
Egg toys, lots of the time; (b) listen to the Puppini Sisters, often;
(c) read the Koran properly rather than making up bits about
murder just because you are a sociopath and are jealous of those
of us who can have a drink. **Euan Ferguson**, in the *Observer*, 24 September 2006

Our religion, such as it is, has abandoned the only territory where
it could not be challenged – the saving of souls, and given up
troubling our individual consciences. Instead, it has joined in the
nationalization of the human conscience, so that a man's moral
worth is now measured by the level of taxation he is willing to
support, rather than by his faith or
even his good works. Other
tests – opposition to apartheid
or General Pinochet – are
valued more highly than
personal adherence to the
Ten Commandments or the
Sermon on the Mount. An
adulterer, with the correct
view on Nelson Mandela, is
preferable to a Mother Teresa

**Read the Koran
properly rather
than making
up bits about
murder just
because you are
a sociopath**

who fails to criticize the currently unfashionable regimes of the world. **Peter Hitchens,** *The Abolition of Britain* (1999)

God once had Bach and Michelangelo on his side, he had Mozart, and now who does he have?

If there were ever a God he has lost all possible taste. You've only got to look – forget the aggression and unpleasantness of the radical right or the Islamic hordes to the East – the sheer lack of intelligence and insight and ability to express themselves and to enthuse others of the priesthood and the clerisy here, in this country, and indeed in Europe, you know God once had Bach and Michelangelo on his side, he had Mozart, and now who does he have? People with ginger whiskers and tinted spectacles who reduce the glories of theology to a kind of sharing, you know? That's what religion has become, a feeble and anaemic nonsense … **Stephen Fry,** debating blasphemy with Christopher Hitchens at the Hay-on-Wye Festival, 2005

Religion is more dangerous than an elephant on cocaine wearing high heels

If you believe, as I do, that religion is more dangerous than an elephant on cocaine wearing high heels in Legoland, the invention of religion is a very black mark against the creators of football. In the dock we have Abraham of Ur Kasdim representing Judaism, 'St' Paul of Tarsus and Joshua of Nazareth in the Catholic – later Protestant and

Catholic – corner and Muhammad bringing up the rear for
Islam, holding the hand of the nine-year-old child he married.
We also have L. Ron Hubbard (Scientology), the cravat-wearing
author of *Buckskin Brigades*, and our current Pope, who thinks
men who kiss men are devilish. He expounds this idea while
dressed as Father Christmas. Spirituality,
you say? Congratulations, boys,
on the greatest bullshit ever told.

Tanya Gold, 'Face it, guys, we'd be better off
without you'; in the *Guardian*, 9 July 2009

Republicans You sons of
bitches. I just hate you. I hate you
to the depths of my soul. I will hate
you when I'm dead. I will hate you a
million years after I'm dead. I will still
hate you. My hate will be a star in the firmament that will shine
down on your Republican asses forever. That's how deep this
hatred is, because of what you're doing to this country. Ooh, did
I say all that? Liberal US talk-show host **Mike Malloy**

*You sons
of bitches.
I just hate
you ...*

They were fascinated with Clinton's penis, and they never got a
chance to see it, which is all they wanted. They wanted Clinton
to have to disrobe in a court of law during the deposition that
he had to give for the Paula Jones case. They didn't get a chance
to see his penis. All Republican men are hooked on Viagra ...
Levitra, Cialis. These are what Republican men need in order
to get an erection. And it's because they never got a chance to
see Clinton's penis. Now they have transferred that to Hillary
[Clinton]'s vagina. They are desperate to see Hillary's vagina.

They must … they are fascinated with Hillary as a bitch goddess of some sort, and they want to worship at the vagina. They are sick, sick people … **Mike Malloy**

Ring Tones

I saw an advert on television the other night, exhorting the viewer to download (whatever that means) from the internet (whatever that is) some ring-tones from the latest charts (whatever they are.) A ring-tone is apparently the noise one's mobile phone makes when it rings. What amazed me about this ad was that it started with the question: 'Are you embarrassed by your ring-tone?' Is it possible that there is such a person on the planet? Someone who has such a pathetically low opinion of themselves, someone who is so lacking in personality and brains, someone so vain, shallow and dim, that they would give a shit what other people thought of their ring-tones? **Rory McGrath**, grumpieroldmen.co.uk, 27 April 2005

Anne Robinson
Presenter of *The Weakest Link* She comes over here, this awful woman dressed in black like a ghastly, sadistic schoolteacher. I hate her and I hate her show because it's just an act. **Simon Cowell**, interviewed for the US website post-gazette.com, 26 June 2002

Rocket and Shaved Parmesan
Rocket and shaved Parmesan is not a meal. It is an odour. It should be bundled into a sock and chased by fervid widdling hounds. **Euan Ferguson**, in the *Observer*, 24 September 2006

Rock Music
It's not music, it's a disease. **Mitch Miller**, head of A&R at Columbia Records in the 1950s and early 1960s

It's not music, it's a disease

'Rock' … is the expression of elemental passions, and at rock festivals it assumes a cultic character, a form of worship, in fact, in opposition to Christian worship. People are, so to speak, released from themselves by the experience of being part of a crowd and by the emotional shock of rhythm, noise, and special lighting effects. However, in the ecstasy of having all their defences torn down, the participants sink, as it were, beneath the elemental force of the universe. **Pope Benedict XVI** gets down and dirty with the youth of today

It's disgusting, it's revolting, it's sheer aggressive sickness, but I don't waste my time fulminating against it because what's the use? What bothers me more than punk rock is supposedly 'intellectual rock'. When people start telling me that Talking

Not just the future of football, but the future of Chavvery

Heads is something very special or when some reputable critic tells me that Dylan is a great poet, that's when my dander is up, because I think it's all junk. **John Simon**, US critic, 1987

Wayne Rooney English footballer King of the boy Chavs
… Picture him screaming 'You fucking ****!' at a referee with a spotty face (Rooney, not the referee) or chewing gum on BBC Sports Personality of the Year awards with a fat, skew-whiff tie. Not just the future of football, but the future of Chavvery.
'The Premiership Chav IX', on Football365.com, 2004

Unlike the fancy-pants multilinguals at Arsenal and Chelsea he looks more like a fan than the fans do … he has the potato face and awful hair and the clamorous family that they have.
Justin Cartwright, in the *Evening Standard*, 25 June 2004

The Battle of the Boobs:
A Supreme Takes on Security

In 1999 at Heathrow Diana Ross, former singer with the Supremes, objected to being frisked by a female security officer, and in retaliation touched the woman's breasts, shouting:

No one touches my breasts! How do you like it? This is how it feels to be fondled. I'm absolutely furious. Do you know when they search you, they actually touch your breast? It's disgraceful. They wouldn't touch a man's penis, would they?

I'm absolutely furious

The star was arrested and cautioned, but not charged.

Jonathan Ross TV and radio presenter Over-excited chat-
show host with a mind like a bowel disease. He can think quicker
than you can flush the chain. **Hermione Eyre** and **William Donaldson**,
The Dictionary of National Celebrity (2005)

Demis Roussos Greek singer Fat, shaggy, rich …
His music … is derivative to the point of putrefaction …
His singing is an unrelenting ying-tong tremolo which would
curdle your brains like paint-stripper if you gave it time.
Clive James, in the *Observer*, 1976

The Royal Family There has to be something wrong
with an institution which assembles, in various degrees of
competitive abjectness, Lord St John of Fawsley, in whom I have
real difficulty believing, Sir Alastair Burnet and Lord Rees-Mogg.
These Firbankian grotesques, prime fruits of the tree of deference,
can be relied on to squelch noisily under royal foot. Happy calling
someone twenty years younger 'Sir' or 'Maa-am', they proclaim
a social pyramid in which their own status is secured by guileful
proximity to the apex. They fawn and teach us to fawn … Such
courtiers only echo the sick adoration of the nation. Royalty has
done a roaring trade since the war in glossy
iconic tosh, books about royal lives,
houses, tours, weddings, ancestry and
interior décor, books, God help us,
about royal dogs. The appetite of silly
people for living vicarious, deferential
lives through this assembly of low-
octane duds in jodhpurs is tragic. **Edward
Pearce**, 'The Aspirin of the People', in the *Guardian*

*This
assembly of
low-octane
duds in
jodhpurs*

The Russians *Racial characteristics:* brutish, dumpy, boorish lard-bags in cardboard double-breasted suits. Lickspittle slaveys to the maniacal schemes of their blood-lusting Red overlords. They make bicycles out of cement and can be sent to Siberia for listening to the wrong radio station. **P.J. O'Rourke**, 'Foreigners Around the World', in *National Lampoon* (1976)

RyanAir Anyone who's ever flown RyanAir knows that its management are cost-cutting pricks who have nothing but contempt for their passengers, headed by the prick-in-chief, Michael O'Leary … **Michael Bywater**, Lost Worlds blog, 5 December 2006

You are not getting a refund so fuck off

O'Leary has said of himself:
I don't give a shit if no one likes me.

O'Leary on the company's no-refund policy:
What part of no refund don't you understand? You are not getting a refund so fuck off. Quoted in the *Guardian*, 4 June 2009

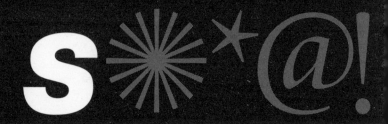

From
Scotland
to
Switzerland

Scotland and the Scots
We're ruled by effete arseholes. What does that make us? The lowest of the fuckin low, the scum of the earth. The most wretched, servile, miserable pathetic trash that was ever shat intae creation. Ah don't hate the English. They just git oan wi the shite thuv goat. Ah hate the Scots. **Irvine Welsh**, *Trainspotting* (1993)

Racial characteristics: sour, stingy, depressing beggars who parade around in schoolgirls' skirts with nothing on underneath. Their fumbled attempt at speaking the English language has been a source of amusement for five centuries, and their idiot music has been dreaded by those not blessed with deafness for at least as long. **P.J. O'Rourke**, 'Foreigners Around the World', in *National Lampoon*, 1976

What does that make us? The lowest of the fuckin low ...

There was a time when if anyone had the impertinence to subject us to the kind of ridicule that has become run of the mill we would have caused an affray, but now we just join in … We have lost our passion. We are like a neutered dog, cowering and waiting to be kicked when not so long ago we would have bitten their bollocks off. **Nicky Campbell** on the decline of Scotland as a footballing nation; in the *Guardian*, 8 December 2005

Brian Sewell
Art critic and scourge of modern art He sounds like a dowager duchess carefully recalling a large turd she was once mistakenly served during tea at Claridge's. **Rachel Cooke**, in the *Observer*, 13 November 2005

Brian Sewell is a fool. Pop artist and Royal Academician **Peter Blake**, quoted in the *Independent on Sunday*, 20 November 2005

We all think it's been absolute hell working with you. **Member of the crew** on Sewell's TV series on the Grand Tour, quoted in the *Observer*, 13 November 2005

He sounds like a dowager duchess carefully recalling a large turd ...

Sex and the City Every time you think there might be a Roy Jones, Jr. fight on HBO, there's Carrie Bradshaw and her gaggle of nervous, self-hating bourgeois Manhattan sluts fretting about their latest three-month relationship that may or may not turn into marriage. America took all the fun out of sex years ago by talking about it publicly so much; now we have shows that talk about talking about sex. It's a wonder any man in Manhattan can ever get an erection. *The Beast's* '50 Most Loathsome People in America 2002'

Alan Shearer English footballer Your legs have gone. You're too old. You're too slow. You couldn't even kiss my arse. Text from **Craig Bellamy** to Shearer, quoted in the *Independent on Sunday*, 16 May 2005. Shearer retorted that if Bellamy ever showed his face in Newcastle again he would 'knock his block off'.

On Alan Shearer's autobiography, *My Story So Far* (1998):
A tome so devoid of character you could almost see it turning back into plant life. *The Rough Guide to Cult Football* (2003)

Singapore A country the size of a piece of snot.
Chen Tan-Sun, foreign minister of Taiwan

Single Mothers Our human stock is threatened …
a high and rising proportion of children are being born to mothers
least fitted to bring children into the world and bring them up.
They are born to mothers who were first pregnant in adolescence
in social classes 4 and 5. Many of these girls are unmarried,
many are deserted or divorced or soon will be. Some are of low
intelligence, most of low educational attainment … They are
producing problem children, the future unmarried mothers,
delinquents, denizens of our borstals, sub-
normal educational establishments,
prisons, hostels for drifters … If we do
nothing, the nation moves towards
degeneration … The worship of
instinct, of spontaneity, the rejection
of self-discipline, is not progress –
it is degeneration. **Sir Keith Joseph**, speaking
in 1974 as Conservative spokesman on home affairs

If we do nothing, the nation moves towards degeneration

Smoking and Anti-Smoking

Smoking is, as far as I am concerned, the entire point of being
an adult. Many people find smoking objectionable. I myself find
many – even more – things objectionable. I do not like aftershave
lotion, adults who roller-skate, children who can speak French, or
anyone who is unduly tan. I do not, however, go around enacting
legislation and putting up signs. **Fran Lebowitz**

In modern-day, New Age America folks would prefer that your
dog vomit on the new Karastan than that you ignite a Don Diego
Lonsdale in their presence. In their vicinity. In their lifetime.
Bruce McCall

© page 251

Arseholes of Scotland ⟩⟩

Dundee Scumdee, the Great Unwashed, the tinks from doon the Tay … Worst city on this planet. Famous for prisoners at Forfar jail preferring to stay in prison than visit it for a day-trip. Populated by subsidy junkies, tinks, soap-dodgers, coagies, etc., all financed by the charitable folk in Perth. A supporter of St Johnstone FC, the Perth club, on www.grange.demon.co.uk

Edinburgh A wet, miserable, Scotch-bastard place only made tolerable by a substantial heroin habit. Hermione Eyre and William Donaldson, *The Dictionary of National Celebrity* (2005)

Glasgow It may be a corpse, but the maggot-swarm upon it is very fiercely alive. One cannot watch and hear the long beat of traffic down Sauchiehall Street, or see its eddy and spume where St Vincent Street and Renfield Street cross, without realizing what excellent grounds the old-fashioned anthropologist appeared to have for believing that man was by nature a brutish savage, a herd-beast delighting in vocal discordance and orgiastic aural abandon. Lewis Grassic Gibbon, 'Glasgow'

The average Glasgow guy now looks like he spends more time in front of the mirror than a pubescent girl. You know what? If you're going to spend two hours on your appearance every day why not work out, you fat fucks? If you're going to have a haircut that makes you look like a moderately powerful Pokemon, try to make sure your body doesn't look like something that's just been fished out of a river. Frankie Boyle

Of the smoking ban in Ireland:

I don't think I'm exaggerating, do you, to call it the worst thing that has ever happened in the whole history of civilization.

Anthony Bourdain, celebrity chef, interviewed in the *Observer*, 30 April 2006

Pubs are just plain wrong without smoking. For all the alcohol, without fags, they have the atmosphere of a 1950s Soviet tea dance. People who prefer pubs smokeless are the same people no one wants to drink with anyway, prissy bores taking umbrage at 'going home smelling like an ashtray'. As if their hideous aftershaves and perfumes aren't offensive to decent smokers …

Barbara Ellen, in the *Observer*, 17 May 2009

One thing I like about Bloody Mary: She never nagged her subjects about lung cancer. I would much rather be at the mercy of someone with the power to say, 'Off with her head!' than be nibbled to death by a bureaucratic duck.   **Florence King**, 'the thinking man's redneck', 1992

South Koreans

Too busy eating dogs to design a decent car.   **Jeremy Clarkson**, October 1998

Spain   The Spanish wine, my God, it is foul, catpiss is champagne compared, this is the sulphurous urination of some aged horse.   **D.H. Lawrence**, letter from Palma to Rhys Davis, 25 April 1929

➲ page 256

The sulphurous urination of some aged horse

Snouts in the Trough

The revelations in May 2009 of the claims being entered by Westminster MPs under their second-home allowance scheme led to widespread public outrage.

Theirs is a larcenous land of loopholes, exemptions, expenses, allowances and shameless fiddles, which spits in the face of every honest British taxpayer … There are so many snouts in the trough that you'd be forgiven for thinking that a swine flu epidemic had broken out at Westminster. **Richard Littlejohn**, in the *Daily Mail*, 9 May 2009

Until … politicians realize taxpayers are their masters not their benefactors we will continue to have a parliament of petty pick-pockets … Dave [Cameron] said sorry last night … Gordon [Brown] has just jumped on the apology bandwagon: 'I want to apologise on behalf of politicians … we must have the highest standards for our profession.' Politics is not a profession, Gordon, it is a racket, and this has been going on for decades not days. Guido won't believe they are sorry until they pay back the money they have embezzled. Then they will be really sorry … **'Guido Fawkes'** blog, 11 May 2009

Voters will not be fobbed off with cosmetic reforms. They want this sewer steam-cleaned – top to bottom. **The *Sun***, 12 May 2009

Like sheep [MPs] all went along with these scams, so that's supposed to make them all right. 'It wasn't my fault, m'lud, that I claimed for a barbecue – it was the system.' Sounds awfully like 'I was only obeying orders' in another era. In a kind of spivs' chorus, they whine in unison that it was all 'within the rules'. But rules can be manipulated for corrupt or otherwise indefensible ends. **Melanie Phillips**, in the *Daily Mail*, 12 May 2009

You'd be forgiven for thinking that a swine flu epidemic had broken out at Westminster

Snouts in the Trough (continued)

Winston Churchill called Westminster the 'shrine of the world's liberties'. I wonder what the old man would make of the vile little snake-pit of ruthless greed our once venerable Palace has become ... My dad and thousands more like him gave the best years of their lives to fight and win a war which maintained our democracy. Is this the calibre of politician they deserve? ... While we work hard to pay food bills, mortgages and council tax the superannuated freeloaders of Westminster can rely on their homes to be furnished, their pensions pumped up and stamp duty to be paid courtesy of the state ... It might help if they displayed just the teensiest hint of remorse. Not this cacophony of protest, denial, buck-passing and blame ... These politicians – jumping around like demented meerkats because we've suddenly become privy to their dirty little secrets – are the very same ones who have spent years exercising a Kremlin-like determination to pry into our lives. **Sue Carroll** in the *Daily Mirror*, 12 May 2009

There is probably more integrity inside Wormwood Scrubs prison than inside the Commons. The traditional ethic of public service has been replaced by the new creed of fleecing the public, as self-enrichment becomes the key political activity of far too many members.

This culture of grubby avarice

So widespread is this culture of grubby avarice that MPs expect taxpayers to underwrite their purchase of chocolate, Christmas trees, soft furnishings, televisions, and even lavatory seats. I'm surprised that Gordon Brown has not put in an expenses claim for his renowned moral compass. **Leo McKinstry**, in the *Daily Express*, 11 May 2009

On attempts by Speaker Michael Martin to defend MPs' snouts in the collective trough, and his attacks on MPs who were critical of the gravy-train culture:

The people want blood

The mask came off Commons Speaker Michael Martin … and the country had a chance to see this bent, bullying berk for what he is: a purple-faced disaster for democracy. Boy, he lost it. Gobblin', gabbling Gorbals Mick! … What followed was a puce-cheeked , finger-wagging, dooon't-you-cross-me-Jimmy tantrum, improper from any chairman of any parish meeting let alone the Speaker of the Commons in crisis … It was the convulsive panic of a Pooh-Bah martinet, nerves as frayed as David Niven's dressing gown cord … He had begun by reading, badly, a typed statement … A Speaker who can barely speak. Says it all, really … He told MPs they must bear in mind 'the spirit of what is right'. Ha! Coming from him that's as ripe as a black banana … This from a quivering incompetent … If he didn't claim to be teetotal you might have suspected he had a raging whisky hangover. But given that he doesn't take a dram, we can but conclude he had overdosed on bile … He deserves every shovel of manure that will now no doubt be hurled at him. **Quentin Letts**, in the *Daily Mail*, 12 May 2009. Martin resigned a week later.

Politicians? Pass me the machine gun … ministers keep telling us that 'what the people really want' is for them to get on with the job, without bothering to consult us. If I hear 'what the people really want' again, I'm reaching for the AK47. The people want blood, they want bodies … This corrupt bunch of co-conspirators have no interest other than hanging onto their own pay, perks and power for as long as possible … **Richard Littlejohn**, in the *Mail Online*, 23 May 2009

The meal was of course filthy. It began with glazed seafood and continued with ridiculously tough veal or something, the whole washed down with vile wine. Spanish food and drink were never up to much in my experience, but you used to be able to depend on simplicities like tomatoes, onions, olives, oranges and the local red. Not now. **Kingsley Amis**, 'Amis Abroad', in the *Spectator*, 23 November 1963

Britney Spears US singer A delusional … hick who, by
talent alone, should be a day-shift stripper … **IDon'tLikeYouInThatWay.com**

Special Offers How about those manufacturers'
coupons featuring Exciting Offers wherein it turns out, when you read the fine print, that you have to send in the coupon *plus* proof of purchase *plus* your complete dental records by registered mail to Greenland and allow at least 18 months for them to send you *another* coupon that will entitle you to 29 cents off your next purchase of a product you don't really want? **Dave Barry**

Sylvester Stallone US actor His diction (always bad) is
now incomprehensible, as if his ego has grown so big that it now fills his mouth like a cup of mashed potatoes. **John Powers**

Stupidity Think of how stupid the average person is, and
realize half of them are stupider than that. **George Carlin**, US comedian

Some scientists claim that hydrogen, because it is so plentiful, is the basic building block of the universe. I dispute that. I say there is more stupidity than hydrogen, and that is the basic building block of the universe. **Frank Zappa** (with Peter Occhiogrosso), *The Real Frank Zappa Book* (1989)

Alan Sugar Entrepreneur and one-time chairman of Tottenham Hotspur

Sir Alan Sugar comes across on TV as exactly the sort of cock who Tory voters like. His brand of 'no-nonsense' nonsense and second-hand rhetoric, and his public affirmation that wealth makes what you say more important, are perfectly judged to appeal to the sort of idiot who thinks David Cameron talks of lot of sense … **David Mitchell**, in the *Observer*, 14 June 2009

The Sun (Not the newspaper)

I too find my spirits lift when the sun emerges but unlike others I am not afraid to say that I think the sun is a stupid bastard. It could so easily make us happy yet continues its conspiracy with the clouds to prevent this happening … You cannot look at the sun directly. Why not? What has it got to hide? … The sun can fuck right off. **Arthur Smith**

They're slowly boring themselves to death

Sunbathing

I don't understand that stuff at all. You go to the beach and you see people just *lying* there. Read a book! Read a magazine! Go swimming! What are you, a plant? **Ian Shoales**, US humorist, 1987

The Swedes

Racial characteristics: tedious, clean-living boy scout types, strangers to graffiti and littering but who are possessed of an odd suicidal mania. Speculation is that they're slowly boring themselves to death. This is certainly the case if their cars and movies are any indication. **P.J. O'Rourke**, 'Foreigners Around the World', in *National Lampoon*, 1976

Stupidity ...
the basic
building
block of the
universe

Referring to the appointment of Sven-Göran Eriksson as manager of England:
We've sold our birthright down the fjord to a nation of seven million skiers and hammer throwers who spend half their lives in darkness. **The *Daily Mail*, in 2000**

Switzerland and the Swiss
What a bloody country! Even the cheese has got holes in it. **Tom Stoppard**, *Travesties* (1975)

The only nation I've ever been tempted to feel really racist about are the Swiss – a whole country of phobic handwashers living in a giant Barclays Bank. **Jonathan Raban**, *Arabia through the Looking Glass* (1979)

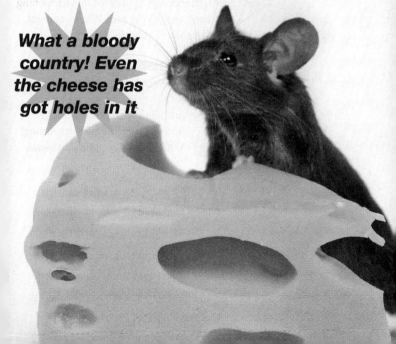

What a bloody country! Even the cheese has got holes in it

From
Technophobes
to
Tyson

Technophobes

Of computers:

I don't know how to plug the things in. I'm scared of electricity, actually. Every time I plug something in, I think I'm going to die. I'm scared to turn the heat on right now because I'm afraid the house will blow up. **John Waters**, 1992

In a world which is run more and more through technology, the sort of chap who says 'Oh, I barely know how to turn the damn thing on, let alone how it works' seems less like the elevated being he imagines himself to be, and more like an idiot, in both the modern and the ancient Athenian senses of the word. **Michael Bywater**, Lost Worlds blog, 21 March 2007

Telethons The spectacle

of all that self-congratulatory yap masquerading as conscience, of all those chairmen of the board passing off public relations as altruism is truly sickening. **Harry Stein**

> *All those chairmen of the board passing off public relations as altruism is truly sickening*

Television Listen to me! Television is not

the truth. Television's a goddamn amusement park. Television is a circus, a carnival, a travelling troupe of acrobats, storytellers, dancers, singers, jugglers, sideshow freaks, lion tamers and football players. We're in the boredom-killing business. So if you want the truth, go to God. Go to your gurus. Go to yourselves, because that's the only place you're going to find any real truth. But, man, you're never gonna get any truth from us. We'll tell you anything you wanna hear. We lie like hell … We'll tell you any shit you want to hear. We deal in illusions, man. None of it is true! But … you're beginning to think that the tube is reality and that your own lives are unreal. … This is mass madness you maniacs! In God's name you people are the real thing, WE are the illusion! **Howard Beale**, anchor of a fictional TV network, played by Peter Finch in the film *Network* (1976)

Oh dear. What a terrible trade we work in. *Blue Peter* is bent. *Five* is a faker. *Richard and Judy's* competitions give a glorious new meaning to their slogan 'You say, we pay.' (They did, to the tune of hundreds of thousands of pounds.) *Big Brother* gets castigated for being an exploitative freak show. (Sorry, what's the story there, then?) The ITV press office misrepresents a documentary. Channel Four's *Born Survivor* Bear Grylls turns out to need Room Service. *Even Children in Need*, and *Comic Relief*, turn out to be guilty of something worse than insufferable smugness. The Prime Minister is mad at us. Even the Queen is cross. And that great Alpha Male, Gordon Ramsay can't even catch his own fucking fish. **Jeremy Paxman**, opening words of his James MacTaggart memorial lecture at the Media Guardian Edinburgh International Television Festival, August 2007

Blue Peter is bent

Televised sport I firmly believe all sport should be tucked away on pay-to-view satellite channels, not smeared across the public broadcast schedules like brown goo in a dirty protest. OK, this policy is founded on personal prejudice – I HATE SPORT and football is the worst offender – but I'm in charge now, so we're getting rid of it. Actually, no – we'll still show it, but in a form that'll deliberately enrage the fans – by superimposing an obtuse east European cartoon over the footage, accompanied by the sound of loud, atonal trumpets. Consider it retribution for the years of tedium and bellowing I've had to endure from the fans, every single one of whom is a despicable idiot. **Charlie Brooker** suggests ways to improve the BBC, in the *Guardian*, 29 May 2004

I HATE SPORT – and football is the worst offender

Tennis and Tennis Players

Tennis players are a load of wankers. I'd love to put John McEnroe in the centre for Fulham [Rugby League Club] and let some of the big players sort him out. **Colin Welland**, in 1980

Eighty per cent of the top women tennis players are fat pigs. Dutch tennis player **Richard Krajicek**, in 1992. He later conceded that he might have exaggerated: 'It's only 75 per cent'.

Mother Teresa Catholic nun Years ago, I did a White House
Correspondents' Dinner, and it was when Reagan was in office.
I said Nancy Reagan had won the Humanitarian of the Year
award. I'm so glad she beat out that conniving little bitch Mother
Teresa. **Jay Leno**, interviewed in *LA Weekly*, 16 September 2004

Mother Teresa of Calcutta was a fanatical
fundamentalist, and, indeed, she took
the most extreme line, a line far more
extreme than her own church, on all
matters – of economics, of morality, of
politics, of authority. And proselytizing
among helpless people, trying to bribe
them with handfuls of rice; praising the
Duvalier family [the Haitian dictators Papa and Baby Doc] because
it stood up for the Catholic interest in Haiti; fawning on Nancy
Reagan … all this was right there for anyone to see. They wouldn't
see it, though, because, 'No, no she's a saint, she's doing work with
the poor …' **Christopher Hitchens**, in conversation with Harry Kreisler at the Institute of
International Studies, University of California, Berkeley, 25 April 2002

*That
conniving
little bitch*

Margaret Thatcher Former Conservative prime minister
She seems to derive more pleasure from admiring new missiles
than great works of art. What else can we expect from an ex-Spam
hoarder from Grantham presiding over the social and economic
decline of the country. **Tony Banks**, Labour MP

What does she want, this housewife, my balls on a tray? **Jacques Chirac**,
then French prime minister, referring to Margaret Thatcher at an EU summit in Brussels,
February 1988

She behaves with all the sensitivity
of a sex-starved boa constrictor.
Tony Banks MP

*Repulsive
in almost
every way*

That Thatcher woman! She has the eyes
of Caligula, but the mouth of Marilyn
Monroe. **President François Mitterrand**

Loathsome, repulsive in almost every way. **Jonathan Miller**

La Pasionara of middle-class privilege … Pétain in petticoats …
Rhoda the Rhino … She approaches the problems of our country
with all the one-dimensional subtlety of a comic strip. **Denis Healey,**
former Deputy Leader of the Labour Party, remarks on various occasions

The Theatre
Stage-plays … are sinful, heathenish, lewd,
ungodly spectacles, and most pernicious corruptions; condemned
in all ages as intolerable mischiefs to churches, republics, to the
manners, minds and souls of men. And that the profession of
play-poets, of stage-players, together with the penning, acting
and frequenting of stage-plays, are unlawful, infamous and
misbeseeming Christians. **William Prynne** (1600–69), English puritan

Tories
They are nothing else but a load of kippers – two-faced,
with no guts. **Eric Heffer**, Labour MP

And the Tories now with their pitiful relaunch – oh, Michael
Howard, we're supposed to have forgotten him from before because
he's had this Trinny and Susannah makeover and you imagine them
with him saying, 'We think you'll like what we've done, Michael, just
have a little look in the mirror – Oh no, you can't really, can you?

We've stitched you a lovely little shadow on – we think you'll really like that.' Ann Widdecombe's confused us all by going blonde – I was watching *Question Time* for half an hour, thinking Christ, Sue Barker's slapped on a bit of weight! **Linda Smith**, *Wrap Up Warm* tour, May 2004

In descending order of vehemence, my objections to the Tory species stem from (a) everything they do, (b) everything they say, (c) everything they stand for, (d) how they look, (e) their stupid names and (f) the noises I imagine they make in bed … The Conservative party is an eternally irritating force for wrong that appeals exclusively to bigots, toffs, money-minded machine men, faded entertainers and selfish, grasping simpletons who were born with some essential part of their soul missing. None of history's truly historical figures has been a Tory, apart from the ones that were, and they only did it by mistake. **Charlie Brooker**, in the *Guardian*, 2 April 2007

Appeals exclusively to bigots, toffs, faded entertainers and selfish, grasping simpletons

I notice from the papers and on television today that the Tories have now brought in a new person to get people to vote Tory, and I could not help noticing that the person is named, as I saw on the website, 'Mr Tosser'. I do not know which person on the Front Bench this man is modelled on, but let me tell the Right Hon. Gentleman that I always thought that his party was full of them, and that is why they have lost three elections. **John Prescott**, speech in the House of Commons, 29 November 2006

The only way you can ever accuse a Conservative of hypocrisy is if they walk past a homeless person without kicking him in the face. **Jeremy Hardy**, on *The News Quiz*, November 2008

Tourists

Tourism is just national prostitution. We don't need any more tourists. They ruin cities. **Prince Philip**, remark to Dr Maja Uran during a visit to Slovenia, 2008

The roads of West Somerset are jammed as never before with caravans from Birmingham and the West Midlands. Their horrible occupants only come down here to search for a place where they can go to the lavatory free. Then they return to Birmingham, boasting in their hideous flat voices how much money they have saved ... Few of these repulsive creatures in caravans are Christians, I imagine, but I would happily spend the rest of my days composing epitaphs for them in exchange for a suitable fee:

> *He had a shit on Gwennap Head,*
> *It cost him nothing. Now he's dead.*
> *He left a turd on Porlock Hill.*
> *As he lies here, it lies there still.*

Auberon Waugh, in *Private Eye*, 11 June 1976

These repulsive creatures in caravans

Train Travel

What was wrong with train toilet doors that just locked, instead of this multiple-choice system? If anything goes wrong, you'll be sitting there while the whole toilet wall slowly slides away, unveiling you like a prize on a quiz show. For 500 points, a shitting woman! **Frankie Boyle**

The train system is so chronic now that any journey you undertake by train in Britain is identical to the one taken by Omar Sharif in *Doctor Zhivago*, that's what it's like – the same drama and misery. Ancient, knackered, rolling stock limping painfully across the land, shuddering to a halt for no apparent reason with the lights flickering on and off – everyone running up and down – 'What's going on?' 'What's up ahead?' I don't know – Is it Rod Steiger with the White Guard? Desperate women in headscarves running alongside the carriages throwing their babies into the train, shouting, 'I'LL NEVER SEE PURLEY OAKS BUT MY CHILD MIGHT!' **Linda Smith**, *Wrap Up Warm* tour, May 2004

Trinny and Susannah

Style gurus You just don't expect posh girls to grab your tits, call your trousers 'too clitty' and use words like 'pussy pelmet' but they do. You are so shocked by what they are saying that by the time you have recovered and thought of something to say they have whipped you out of your jeans and eased you into a Lycra cat suit. **Sarah Bailey**, editor of *Elle*, quoted in the *Guardian*, 22 December 2002

You just don't expect posh girls to grab your tits

Tina Turner

US singer All legs and hair with a mouth that could swallow the whole stadium and the hot-dog stand. **Laura Lee Davies**, in *Time Out*

'Iron' Mike Tyson

US heavyweight boxer

I love to hit people. I love to, Most celebrities are afraid someone's going to attack them. I want someone to attack me. No weapons. Just me and him. I like to beat men and beat them bad … When I fight someone, I want to break his will. I want to take his manhood. I want to rip out his heart and show it to him. Interviewed in *Sports Illustrated*, March 1988

Prior to a bout with Alex Stewart in December 1990:
It's nothing personal, but I'm going to kill this guy.

Talking about his daughter Rayna in March 1996:
Her mother is beautiful, but she is so gorgeous she makes her mother look like a junkyard dog.

After knocking out Jesse Ferguson, quoted in the *New Yorker*, 14 July 1997:
I wanted to hit him one more time in the nose so that bone could go up into his brain.

I want to rip out his heart

On his forthcoming fight with François Botha, 1998:
I think I'll take a bath in his blood … I'm not much for talking. You know what I do. I put guys in body bags when I'm right.

u@!

Just
Underwear

Underwear

Like very large numbers of men in this country I have always bought my socks and pants at Marks & Sparks. I have noticed that something very troubling has happened. There's no other way to put this. Their pants no longer provide adequate support. When I've discussed this with friends and acquaintances it has revealed widespread gusset anxiety. The other thing is socks. Even among those of us who clip our toenails very rigorously they appear to be wearing out much more quickly on the big toe. Also, they're no longer ribbed around the top, which means they do not stay up in the way that they used to. These are matters of great concern to the men of Britain. I just felt it was time that somebody raised this with the only man who can sort it out, Stuart Rose. **Jeremy Paxman**, quoted in *Mail Online*, 20 January 2008. The *Newsnight* presenter raised his concerns about the nation's underwear in an e-mail to Sir Stuart Rose, chief executive of Marks & Spencer.

It has revealed widespread gusset anxiety

V@!

From
Van Damme
to
Vegetarians

Jean-Claude Van Damme Belgian actor ['The Muscles from Brussels'] He might not be French, but he speaks it, and has a stupid French name. Oh yeah, one more thing. Worst. Actor. Ever.
France sucks.net

Vegetarians Milky-faced do-gooders who are so malnourished that their brains are incapable of telling the difference between what is music and what is a wind chime.
Hadley Freeman (herself a vegetarian), in the *Guardian*, 17 June 2009

My biggest nightmare would be if the kids ever came up to me and said, 'Dad, I'm a vegetarian.' Then I would sit them on the fence and electrocute them ... **Gordon Ramsay**, quoted in the *Daily Mail*, 29 August 2008

Why not try our vegetarian option? You can fuck off. **Frankie Boyle**

If we aren't supposed to eat animals, then why are they made out of meat? **Jo Brand**

Eating people is wrong. It's wrong because people are carnivores, and we don't eat carnivores. The rule is, not more than two steps from the sun: plants eat sunlight, sheep eat plants, we eat sheep. We don't eat wolves, lions, eagles, or dogs and cats unless we have to. But – and here I can tell you're ahead of me – we could eat vegetarians. As part of a balanced approach to environmental apocalypse, we could have vegetarian Mondays. It would be an easy way to cull some of the most annoyingly sanctimonious and whingeingly pitiful people in the world, while doing good at the same time. Two vegans with one stone. And I expect they taste rather good, being compulsively vain hypochondriacs. **A.A. Gill**, in the *Sunday Times*, 28 June 2009

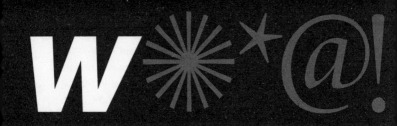

From
**Waffle
waitresses**
to
Word games

Waffle Waitresses   I've noticed a certain anti-
intellectualism going around this country; since about 1980, oddly
enough [*1980 was the year that Ronald Reagan was elected 40th
president of the USA*] … I was in Nashville, Tennessee, and after
the show I went to a Waffle House. I'm not proud of it, but I was
hungry. And I'm sitting there eating and reading a book. I don't
know anybody, I'm alone, so I'm reading a book. The waitress
comes over to me like, [*gum smacking*] 'Wha'chu readin' for?' I
had never been asked that. Not 'What am I *reading*?', but 'What am
I reading *for*?' Goddangit, you stumped me. Hmm, why do I read?
I suppose I read for a lot of reasons, one of the main ones being so
I don't end up being a *fucking waffle waitress*.   US satirist **Bill Hicks**, from
Dangerous (1990)

The Welsh   Fucking Welsh.   **Tony Blair**, in response to Labour's poor
showing in the 1999 Welsh Assembly elections, according to a former press officer quoted in the
Guardian, 19 September 2005

Loquacious dissemblers, immoral liars,
stunted, bigoted, dark, ugly, pugnacious
little trolls.   **A.A. Gill**, in the *Sunday Times*, 1998

The Welsh have never made any
significant contribution to any
branch of knowledge, culture or
entertainment. They have no
architecture, no gastronomic
tradition, no literature
worthy of the name.
A.N. Wilson, *Evening
Standard*, 6 March 1993

*Dark, ugly,
pugnacious
little trolls*

Arseholes of Wales

Cardiff

'We hate Cardiff, we hate Cardiff, we hate Cardiff, we hate Cardiff!' I yell without concession. There is no muttering that despite our general dislike of the capital city we appreciate its superior shopping facilities, that the riverside development is a vital life line for Welsh industry and that, in nearly every way, Cardiff is the cultural hub of Wales. But I digress. 'We hate Cardiff, we hate Cardiff, we hate Cardiff, we hate Cardiff!' **'spack', a Swansea FC supporter, on www.abctales.com**

There isn't a smart hotel in Cardiff. The Grand has one star but that's because it's the only hotel in Cardiff which doesn't nail the furniture to the floor to prevent the guests from stealing it. **Hermione Eyre** and **William Donaldson**, *The Dictionary of National Celebrity* (2005)

'We hate Cardiff, we hate Cardiff, we hate Cardiff, we hate Cardiff!'

Swansea An ashtray of a place, with grids of grey streets and morose neighbourhood pubs frantically competing for the Most Miserable award. *The Lonely Planet Guide to Wales* (2nd edition, 2004)

A vast cankered valley of sorrowful houses and grey churches and shut-down factories … No wonder the Welsh are religious … **Paul Theroux**, *The Kingdom by the Sea* (1983)

The Welsh … What are they for? … irritating and annoying … They are always so pleased with themselves … I never did like them. **Anne Robinson**, consigning the Welsh to oblivion on the popular TV programme *Room 101*, 5 March 2001. After the Welsh police investigated the case for breaches of laws against racism, Robinson apologised.

The Welsh … what are they for?...

Arsène Wenger

Manager of Arsenal FC I think he is one of these – how do you call it in English? – voyeurs. He likes to watch other people. There are some guys, who, when they are at home, they have a big telescope to see what happens in other families. He must be one of them. He speaks and speaks and speaks about Chelsea. **José Mourinho**, then Chelsea manager, accuses Wenger of being obsessed with his club, 29 October 2005

Westlife   Irish boy band A collection of tone-deaf, spud-faced chancers. **Hermione Eyre** and **William Donaldson**, *The Dictionary of National Celebrity* (2005)

Little more than Jerry Springer with a vagina

Oprah Winfrey

US talk show host Little more than Jerry Springer with a vagina. **Scott Marks**, on emulsioncompulsion.com, 17 January 2009

Wives

From the last will and testament of the
Rev. John Forbes, former minister of Sleat
on the Isle of Skye:

Unfortunately addicted to the vice of intemperance

To my beloved wife personally I
cannot entrust anything. Prudence
and my sense of duty forbid it. I
do it with grief and pain, because she has,
during the last 18 years, proved herself utterly unworthy of
trust or confidence, being unfortunately addicted to the vice
of intemperance. Contracting debts without my knowledge
or permission. Imprudent and without any proper regard to
necessary economy. Generally disobedient to the admonitions,
advices and directions which were kindly given to her for her
own best interest, both by myself and by her relatives and friends.
Constantly trying to avoid the vigilance that has been used to
prevent her from going wrong … I earnestly request that there be
very little drinking at my funeral. Quoted by David Mitchell on BBC 1's
Who Do You Think You Are?, 5 August 2009

Naomi Wolf American feminist, author of *The Beauty Myth* Daddy's
little girl … She is so naive. I can't stand her. She's hopeless …
Wolf says we shouldn't succumb to any of this bullshit, but she
spends four hours having makeup applied
before her TV appearances and – I've
heard – can't pass a window without
looking at herself. I mean, look at her
hair! It is the only thing that gave
her cachet when she came onto the
scene. Her book was one of many tired

I can't stand her. She's hopeless …

feminist books. What distinguished her was her hair; she owes everything to that hair. But then she cut it off. She's trying to find a more serious persona. She's looking for a hairstyle. It's horrible. It's embarrassing. **Camille Paglia**, interviewed in *Playboy*, May 1995

Women

Nature, I say, doth paint them further to be weak, frail, impatient, feeble and foolish; and experience hath declared them to be unconstant, variable, cruel and lacking the spirit of counsel and regiment … To promote a woman to bear rule, superiority, dominion or empire above any realm, nation or city, is repugnant to Nature, contumely to God, a thing most contrary to his revealed will and approved ordinance, and finally it is a subversion of good order, of all equity and justice. **John Knox**, *The First Blast of the Trumpet Against the Monstrous Regiment of Women* (1558)

It is only the man whose intellect is clouded by his sexual impulses that could give the name of 'the fair sex' to that undersized, narrow-shouldered, broad-hipped and short-legged race. **Arthur Schopenhauer**

Don't stroke 'em, don't tickle 'em, just give 'em a ruddy good belt

You should treat women the same way as a Yorkshire batsman used to treat a cricket ball. Don't stroke 'em, don't tickle 'em, just give 'em a ruddy good belt. **Fred Trueman**, Yorkshire fast bowler, quoted in David Hopps, *A Century of Great Cricket Quotes* (1998)

Girls today have never had it so good, right? Apart from the fact that you've got more equality than you ever can deal with, the fact of the matter is that you've got real democracy and there are really no glass ceilings, despite the fact that some of you moan about it all the time. Women can get to the top of any single job that they want to in the UK. You've got a woman fighter pilot who went in to join the Red Arrows yesterday. I mean, what else do you want to do, for God's sake? Women astronauts. Women miners. Women dentists. Women doctors. Women managing directors. What is it you haven't got? **Stuart Rose**, executive chairman of Marks and Spencer, interviewed by Elizabeth Day for the *Observer*, 31 May 2009

What else do you want to do, for God's sake?

Needless to say, Rose's rant provoked some strong reactions:
I tell you what I haven't got. Your balls on a plate. **Sandi Toksvig**, on *The News Quiz*, 5 June 2009

Word Games
I always hated TV programmes to do with words. *Call My Bluff, Countdown* – all utterly insufferable. There is a particular kind of word smugness peculiar to the English which is unbearable … It's a cold, soulless fetishizing of words with no regard for their beauty or power. It's a nasty, slimy cleverness that goes down like a cup of cold vomit. It's for the kind of people who think the solving of cryptic clues is the ultimate intellectual endeavour and for whom membership of Mensa is a badge of honour rather than a grubby little secret, belonging to a support group for an underachieving bunch of wankers who like doing puzzles. aerialtelly.co.uk

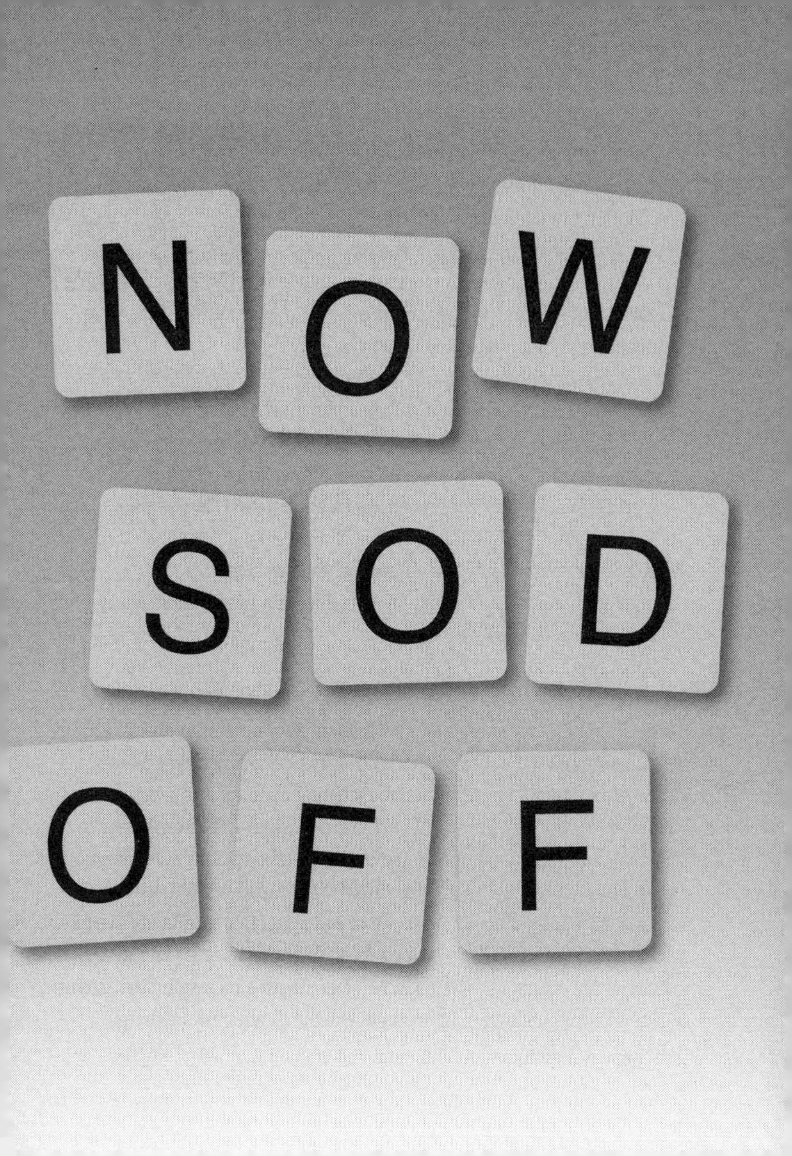
NOW
SOD
OFF

@y!

From
York
to
Youth

Sarah, Duchess of York Former wife of Prince Andrew

She is a lady short on looks, absolutely deprived of any dress sense, has a figure like a Jurassic monster, [seems] very greedy when it comes to loot, no tact and wants to upstage everyone else.

Sir Nicholas Fairbairn MP, in the *Independent*

The Youth of Today Today the world has gone sex

crazy. Illicit sex has become the downfall of many in the Bible. Movie stars not married to each other, having babies and making headlines all over the world as though they were doing some great thing. Big deal! Just another moral pervert. And for them to become heroes for our kids. My wife and I will be married 49 years the next anniversary. **Revd Jerry Falwell**, US televangelist, sermon, 25 June 2006

Plus ça change …

Young men these days? Feckless, brain-dead wasters. Can't be arsed to do anything worthwhile, just lie about like total drips. It's only when they're up to no good that they get off their bloody backsides. What a pack of nancy boys, what with their singing and dancing, their primped hair, their squealing, wheedling, girly voices. With those soft bodies and all that prancing about you'd think they were bloody girls. None of them's got what it takes to call himself a man. They're just a bunch of big babies with no balls. **Seneca the Elder**, *Controversiae*, I (1st century BC), freely translated

Picture credits

Getty Images: 16-17 Pix Inc/Time & Life Pictures, 44-45 Tim Sloan/AFP, 48 Gareth Cattermole, 75 Indigo, 83 Nicholas Kamm/AFP, 86-87 Popperfoto, 116-117 Imagno, 183 Danny Martindale/WireImage, 199 Leon Neal/AFP, 209 Gregg DeGuire/WireImage, 224-225 Kirsty Wigglesworth/AFP, 269 Dennis Kitchen.
Rex Features: 29 Everett Collection, 35, 131, 145, 175, 249 Rex, 57 Brian J.Ritchie, 95 Nick Cunard, 102 Steve Bardens, 119 Darren Seiler/Newspix, 142-143 Paul Greaves, 151 Philip Brown, 179 WestEnd, 218 Andrew Drysdale, 240 Matt Roberts, 265 Julian Makey.
Graham Morris: 71.
Press Association/Empics: 125 Mike Egerton, 160-161 S&G.
Topfoto: 135
Corbis: 214 Reuters
All other images copyright **www.iStockphoto.com**

First published in Great Britain in 2009 by
Quercus
21 Bloomsbury Square
London
WC1A 2NS

A CIP catalogue record for this book is available
from the British Library

ISBN 978 1 84916 124 4

10 9 8 7 6 5 4 3 2 1

Printed in the UK by CPI William Clowes Beccles NR34 7TL

Designed by Martin Anderson
Edited by Peter Lewis
Picture research by Elaine Willis

r✳*@!